SIDE *by* SIDE

CORE CONVERSATION COURSE

SECOND EDITION

BEGINNING

Steven J. Molinsky / Bill Bliss

PRENTICE HALL REGENTS
Englewood Cliffs, New Jersey 07632

Library of Congress Cataloging-in-Publication Data

Molinsky, Steven J.
   Side by side : core conversation course : beginning / Steven J.
Molinsky, Bill Bliss.—2nd ed.
     p. 208
   ISBN 0-13-811860-4
   1. English language—Conversation and phrase books. 2. English
language—Textbooks for foreign speakers. I. Bliss, Bill.
II. Title.
PE1131.M58 1990
428.3′4—dc20   89-37125
                                        CIP

Editorial/production supervision: Noël Vreeland Carter
Art supervision: Meg Van Arsdale
Manufacturing buyer: Peter Havens
Cover design: Karen Stephens

Illustrated by Richard E. Hill

© 1990 by Prentice Hall Regents
Prentice-Hall, Inc.
A Paramount Communications Company
Englewood Cliffs, New Jersey 07632

Printed in the United States of America

10 9 8 7

ISBN 0-13-811860-4

Prentice-Hall International (UK) Limited, *London*
Prentice-Hall of Australia Pty. Limited, *Sydney*
Prentice-Hall Canada Inc., *Toronto*
Prentice-Hall Hispanoamericana, S.A., *Mexico*
Prentice-Hall of India Private Limited, *New Delhi*
Prentice-Hall of Japan, Inc., *Tokyo*
Simon & Schuster Asia Pte. Ltd., *Singapore*
Editora Prentice-Hall do Brasil, Ltda., *Rio de Janeiro*

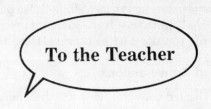

Side by Side Core Conversation Course: Beginning consists of the conversational grammar lessons contained in *Side by Side Second Edition: Books 1 and 2*. It is designed to serve as a supplementary or stand-alone conversation practice book.

The goal of the *Side by Side Core Conversation Course* is to help students learn to use English grammatically, through practice with meaningful conversational exchanges. The text is intended for adult and young-adult learners of English. It is designed to provide the beginning student with the basic foundation of English grammar through a carefully sequenced progression of conversational exercises and activities. Teachers of false-beginning students will also find these materials effective as a rapid, concise review of basic structures of the language.

WHY A CONVERSATIONAL GRAMMAR APPROACH?

Grammar is usually isolated and drilled through a variety of traditional structural exercises such as repetition, substitution, and transformation drills. These exercises effectively highlight particular grammar structures . . . but they are usually presented as a string of single sentences, not related to each other in any unifying, relevant context.

Traditional dialogs, on the other hand, may do a fine job of providing examples of real speech, but they don't usually offer sufficient practice with the structures being taught. Teachers and students are often frustrated by the lack of a clear grammatical focus in these meaningful contexts. And besides that, it's hard to figure out what to *do* with a dialog after you've read it, memorized it, or talked about it.

In the *Side by Side Core Conversation Course*, we have attempted to combine the best features of traditional grammar drills and contextually rich dialogs. We aim to actively engage students in meaningful conversational exchanges within carefully structured grammatical frameworks. And we encourage students to then break away from the text and *use* these frameworks to create conversations *on their own*.

While we have designed this text for the beginning student, we are also concerned about the false-beginner. Although this student has made progress in understanding and using the language, he or she often needs more practice with the basics, the "nuts and bolts" of elementary English grammar. (Teachers of false-beginners often say that even though their students may be doing beautifully with the present perfect tense, they still have trouble with such "early" structures as the third-person singular -*s* or the difference between the simple present and present continuous tenses.) This book offers false-beginners the opportunity to use their richer vocabularies in open-ended conversational exercises that focus on the basic grammatical structures of the language.

AN OVERVIEW

Chapter Opening Pages

The opening page of each chapter provides an overview of the new grammatical structures treated in the chapter.

Grammatical Paradigms

A new grammatical structure appears first in the form of a grammatical paradigm, or "grammar box"—a simple schema of the structure. Grammar boxes are in a light gray tint.

These paradigms are meant to be a reference point for students as they proceed through the lesson's conversational activities. While these paradigms highlight the structures being taught, they are not intended to be goals in themselves. Students are not expected to memorize or parrot back these rules. Rather, we want students to take part in conversations that show they can *use* these rules correctly.

Guided Conversations

Guided conversations are the dialogs and question and answer exchanges which are the primary learning devices in this book. Students are presented with a model conversation that highlights a specific aspect of the grammar. In the exercises that follow the model, students pair up and work "side by side," placing new content into the given conversational framework. These exercises form the core learning activity of each lesson.

On Your Own and How About You? Activities

These student-centered activities give students valuable opportunities to apply lesson content to their own lives and experiences and to share opinions in class. Through these activities, students bring to the classroom new content, based on their interests, their backgrounds, and their imaginations. Activities include role plays, questions about the students' real world, and topics for discussion and debate.

GENERAL TEACHING STRATEGIES

Introducing the Model

There are many alternative ways to introduce the model conversation. We don't want to dictate any particular method. Rather, we encourage you to develop strategies that are compatible with your own teaching style, the specific needs of your students, and the particular grammar and content of the lesson at hand.

Some teachers will want books closed at this stage, so their students will have a chance to listen to the model before seeing it in print. Other teachers will want students to have their books open for the model conversation or see it written on the blackboard. The teacher may play the audio tape, read, or act out the conversation while students follow along, or may read through the model with another student, or may have two students present the model to the class.

Whether books are open or closed, students should have ample opportunity to understand and practice the model before attempting the exercises that follow it.

Side by Side Exercises

In these conversational exercises, we are asking students to place new content into the grammatical and contextual framework of the model. The numbered exercises provide the student with new information which is "plugged into" the framework of the model conversation. Sometimes this framework actually appears as a "skeletal dialog" in the text. Other times the student simply inserts the new information into the model that has just been practiced. (Teachers who have written the model conversation on the board can create the skeletal dialog by erasing the words that are replaced in the exercises.)

The teacher's key function is to pair up students for the "side by side" conversational practice, and then to serve as a resource to the class, for help with the structure, new vocabulary, and pronunciation.

"Side by side" practice can take many forms. Some teachers may prefer to call on two students at a time to present a conversation to the class. Other teachers may want to have all their students pair up and practice the conversations with a partner. Or small groups of students might work together, pairing up within these groups and presenting the conversations to others in the group.

This paired practice helps teachers address the varying levels of ability of their students. Some teachers like to pair stronger students with weaker ones. The slower student clearly gains through this pairing, while the more advanced student also strengthens his or her abilities by lending assistance to the speaking partner. Other teachers will want to pair up or group students of *similar* levels of ability. In this arrangement, the teacher can devote greater attention to students who need it, while giving more capable students the chance to learn from and assist each other.

While these exercises are intended for practice in conversation, teachers also find them useful as *writing* drills which reinforce oral practice and enable students to study more carefully the grammar highlighted in these conversations.

Once again, we encourage you to develop strategies that are most appropriate for your class.

Open-Ended Exercises (the "Blank Box")

In many lessons, the final exercise is an open-ended one. This is indicated in the text by a blank box. Here the students are expected to create conversations based on the structure of the model, but with vocabulary which they select themselves. This provides students with an opportunity for creativity, while still focusing on the particular structure being practiced. These open-ended exercises can be done orally in class and/or assigned as homework for presentation in class the next day. Encourage students to use dictionaries to find new words they want to use.

On Your Own

On Your Own activities offer students the opportunity to contribute content of their own within the grammatical framework of the lesson. You should introduce these activities in class and assign them as homework for presentation in class the next day. In this way, students will automatically review the previous day's grammar while contributing new and inventive content of their own.

These activities are meant for simultaneous grammar reinforcement and vocabulary building. Students should be encouraged to use a dictionary when completing the *On Your Own* activities. In this way, they will not only use the words they know, but the words they would *like* to know in order to really bring their interests, backgrounds, and imaginations into the classroom.

As a result, students will be teaching each other new vocabulary and also sharing a bit of their lives with others in the class.

How About You?

How About You? activities are intended to provide students with additional opportunities to tell about themselves. Have students do these activities in pairs or as a class.

General Guiding Principles for Working with Guided Conversations

1. When doing the exercises, students should practice *speaking* to each other, rather than *reading* to each other. Therefore, while students will need to refer to the text to be able to practice the conversations, they should not read the lines word by word. Rather, they should practice scanning a full line and then look up from the book, and *speak* the line to another person.

2. Throughout, teachers should use the book to teach proper intonation and gesture. (Capitalized words are used to indicate spoken emphasis.) Students should be encouraged to truly *act out* the dialogs in a strong and confident voice.

3. Use of the texts should be as *student-centered* as possible. Modeling by the teacher should be efficient and economical, but students should have every opportunity to model for each other when they are capable of doing so.

4. Vocabulary can and should be effectively taught in the context of the conversation being practiced. Very often it will be possible to grasp the meaning from the conversation or its accompanying illustration. Teachers should spend time drilling vocabulary in isolation *only* if they feel it is absolutely essential.

5. Students need not formally study or be able to produce grammatical rules. The purpose of the text is to engage students in active communication practice that gets them to *use* the language according to these rules.

6. Students should be given every opportunity to apply their own lives and creative contributions to the exercises. This is directly provided for in the blank boxes at the end of many lessons as well as in the *On Your Own* and *How About You?* activities, but teachers can look to *all* exercises with an eye toward expanding them to the real world of the classroom or the students' real lives.

In conclusion, we have attempted to make the study of English grammar a lively and relevant experience for our students. While we hope that we have conveyed to you the substance of our textbook, we also hope that we have conveyed the spirit: that learning the grammar can be conversational . . . student-centered . . . and fun!

Steven J. Molinsky
Bill Bliss

Contents

1 To Be: Introduction   1

2 To Be + Location
Subject Pronouns   5

3 Present Continuous Tense   11

4 To Be: Short Answers
Possessive Adjectives   17

5 To Be:
    Yes/No Questions
    Short Answers
Adjectives
Possessive Nouns   23

6 To Be: Review
Present Continuous Tense: Review
Prepositions of Location   31

7 Prepositions
There Is/There Are
Singular/Plural: Introduction   35

8 Singular/Plural
Adjectives
This/That/These/Those   43

9 Simple Present Tense   51

10 Simple Present Tense:
    Yes/No Questions
    Negatives
    Short Answers   55

11 Object Pronouns
Simple Present Tense: s vs. non-s Endings
Have/Has
Adverbs of Frequency   61

12 Contrast: Simple Present and
    Present Continuous Tenses
Adjectives   67

13 Can
Have to   73

14 Future: Going to
Time Expressions
Want to   79

15 Past Tense:
    Regular Verbs
    Introduction to Irregular Verbs   87

16 Past Tense:
    Yes/No Questions
    Short Answers
    WH-Questions
    More Irregular Verbs
Time Expressions   93

17 To Be: Past Tense   99

18 Like to
Review of Tenses:
    Simple Present
    Simple Past
    Future: Going to
Time Expressions
Indirect Object Pronouns   105

19 Count/Non-Count Nouns   111

20 Partitives
Count/Non-Count Nouns
Imperatives   117

21 Future Tense: Will
Time Expressions
Might   123

22 Comparatives
Should
Possessive Pronouns   **129**

23 Superlatives   **137**

24 Directions   **143**

25 Adverbs
Comparative of Adverbs
Agent Nouns
If-Clauses   **151**

26 Past Continous Tense
Reflexive Pronouns
While-Clauses   **157**

27 Could
Be Able to
Have Got to
Too + Adjective   **163**

28 Must
Must vs. Should
Count/Non-Count Nouns
Past Tense Review   **171**

29 Future Continuous Tense
Time Expressions   **179**

30 Some/Any
Pronoun Review
Verb Tense Review   **187**

APPENDIX

Cardinal and Ordinal Numbers/Irregular Verbs   **197**
Correlation Key to Activity Workbooks   **198**

INDEX   **200**

To Be: Introduction

What's Your Name?

*What's = What is
†235 = two thirty-five
**741–8906 = seven four one – eight nine "oh" six

Answer these questions.

1. What's your name?

   _____

2. What's your address?

   _____

3. What's your phone number?

   _____

4. Where are you from?

   _____

Now ask other students in your class.

ON YOUR OWN: Interview

Interview a famous person. Make up addresses, phone numbers, and cities. Use your imagination. Role play these interviews in class.

A. What's your name?

B. My name is ~~Xglisibot~~ tailoot.

A. 222 _____ address?

B. _____.

A. _____ phone number?

B. _____.

A. Where are you from?

B. _____.

a famous actor

a famous actress

a famous athlete

the president/prime minister of your country

To Be + Location
Subject Pronouns

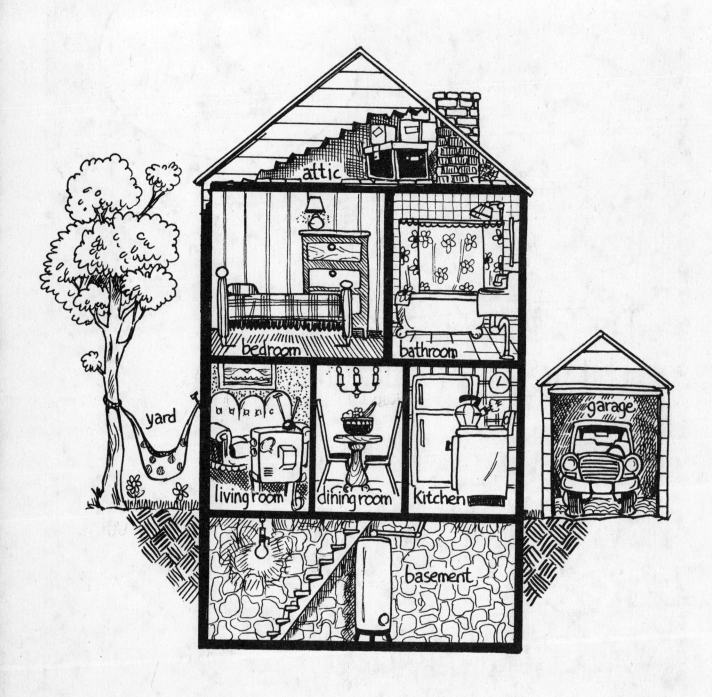

Where Are You?

(I am)	I'm
(He is)	He's
(She is)	She's
(It is)	It's
(We are)	We're
(You are)	You're
(They are)	They're

} in the kitchen.

	am	I
	is	he / she / it
Where		?
	are	we / you / they

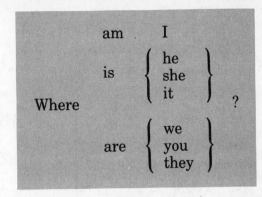

1. Where are you?

2. Where are you?

3. Where are you?

4. Where are you?

5. Where are Bill and Mary?

6. Where are Mr. and Mrs. Wilson?

7. Where are you?

8. Where are you and Tom?

9. Where are Mr. and Mrs. Johnson?

7

Where's Bob?

*Where's = Where is

1. Where's Tom?

2. Where's Fred?

3. Where's Helen?

4. Where's Betty?

5. Where's the newspaper?

6. Where's the cat?

7. Where's Jane?

8. Where's John?

9. Where's the dog?

Where Are They?

Ask and answer questions based on these pictures.

1. _____ Albert?
_____.

2. _____ Carmen?
_____.

3. _____ Walter and Mary?
_____.

4. _____ you?
_____.

5. _____ you?
_____.

6. _____ Rita?
_____.

7. _____ Mr. and Mrs. Jones?
_____.

8. _____ the monkey?
_____.

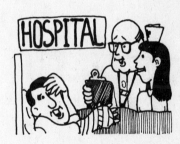

9. _____ I?
_____.

Now add people and places of your own.

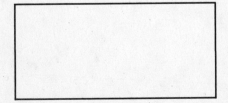

10. _____?
_____.

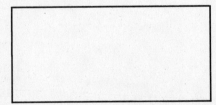

11. _____?
_____.

12. _____?
_____.

Present Continuous Tense

What Are You Doing?

(I am)	I'm	
(He is)	He's	
(She is)	She's	
(It is)	It's	} eating.
(We are)	We're	
(You are)	You're	
(They are)	They're	

	am	I	
What	is	{ he she it }	doing?
	are	{ we you they }	

Complete these conversations.

1. **A.** What are you doing?
   B. _____ reading the newspaper.

2. **A.** _____ Mr. and Mrs. Jones doing?
   B. _____ eating dinner.

3. **A.** _____ Henry doing?
   B. _____ cooking dinner.

4. **A.** _____ Maria doing?
   B. _____ studying English.

5. **A.** _____ Frank doing?
   B. _____ sleeping.

6. **A.** _____ Sam and Betty doing?
   B. _____ watching TV.

7. **A.** _____ Judy doing?
   B. _____ playing the piano.

8. **A.** What are YOU doing?
   B. I'm _____.

13

What's Everybody Doing?

A. Where's Walter?

B. He's in the kitchen.

A. What's he doing?

B. He's eating breakfast.

1. *Betty*
park
eating lunch

2. *Mr. and Mrs. Smith*
dining room
eating dinner

3. *you*
bedroom
playing the guitar

4. *you*
living room
playing cards

5. *Tom and Mary*
yard
playing baseball

6. *Miss Jackson*
restaurant
drinking coffee

7. *Mr. Larson*
cafeteria
drinking lemonade

8. *you*
library
studying English

9. *Tommy*
classroom
studying mathematics

10. *Gloria*
night club
dancing

11. *Harry*
bathroom
singing

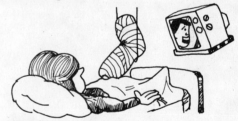

12. *Barbara*
hospital
watching TV

13. *you*
park
listening to the radio

14.

To Be: Short Answers
Possessive Adjectives

I'm Fixing My Sink

I	my
he	his
she	her
it	its
we	our
you	your
they	their

Are You Busy?

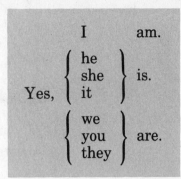

Yes,
I am.
he she it } is.
we you they } are.

1. Is Nancy busy?
washing her car

2. Is Ted busy?
feeding his dog

3. Are you busy?
cleaning our yard

4. Are Mr. and Mrs. Jones busy?
painting their kitchen

5. Are you busy?
doing my homework

6. Is Alan busy?
doing his exercises

7. Is Linda busy?
fixing her bicycle

8. Are you busy?
cleaning our apartment

9. Are Bob and Judy busy?
washing their windows

10. Is Pedro busy?
feeding his cat

11. Are you busy?
washing my clothes

12. Are you busy?
fixing our TV

13. Is Henry busy?
cleaning his garage

14. Are your children busy?
brushing their teeth

Use this model to talk about the picture with other students in your class.

A. Where's Miss Johnson?

B. She's in the parking lot.

A. What's she doing?

B. She's washing her car.

To Be:
   Yes/No Questions
   Short Answers
Adjectives
Possessive Nouns

Tall or Short?

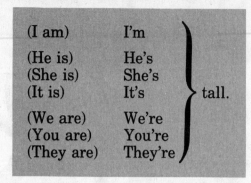

(I am)	I'm
(He is)	He's
(She is)	She's
(It is)	It's
(We are)	We're
(You are)	You're
(They are)	They're

} tall.

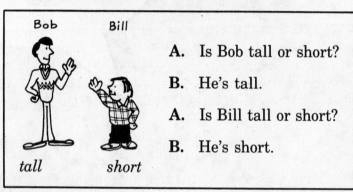

Bob   Bill

tall   *short*

A. Is Bob tall or short?

B. He's tall.

A. Is Bill tall or short?

B. He's short.

Ask and answer these questions.

Alice   Margaret

young   *old*

Herman   David

heavy
fat   *thin*

1. Is Alice young or old?

2. Is Margaret young or old?

3. Is Herman heavy or thin?

4. Is David fat or thin?

Herman's car   David's car

new   *old*

Betty   Hilda

beautiful
pretty   *ugly*

5. Is Herman's car new or old?

6. Is David's car new or old?

7. Is Betty beautiful or ugly?

8. Is Hilda pretty or ugly?

9. Is Edward handsome or ugly?

10. Is Captain Blood handsome or ugly?

11. Is Albert rich or poor?

12. Is John rich or poor?

13. Is Albert's house large or small?

14. Is John's apartment big or little?

15. Are Mary's neighbors noisy or quiet?

16. Are Jane's neighbors loud or quiet?

17. Is champagne expensive or cheap?

18. Is tea expensive or cheap?

19. Is Barbara married or single?

20. Is Julie married or single?

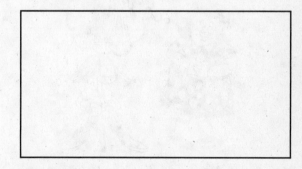

21. Are the questions in Chapter 5 easy or difficult?

22. Are the questions in Chapter 17 easy or difficult?

Now ask and answer questions of your own.

Tell Me About . . .

Am	I				I		am.		I'm		not.
Is	he she it	tall?		Yes,	he she it	}	is.	No,	he she it	}	isn't.
Are	we you they				we you they	}	are		we you they	}	aren't.

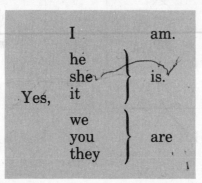

Are you married?

No, I'm not. I'm single.

Tell me about your new car. Is it large?

No, it isn't. It's small.

Tell me about your new neighbors. Are they quiet?

No, they aren't. They're noisy.

1. A. Tell me about your brother.

<u>Yes he</u> <u>is</u> tall?

B. No, _____. _____.

2. A. Tell me about your sister.

<u>Yes she</u> <u>is</u> single?

B. No, _____. _____.

26

3. A. Tell me about your apartment.

_____ _____ new?

B. No, _____. _____.

4. A. Tell me about your new boss.

_____ _____ old?

B. No, _____. _____.

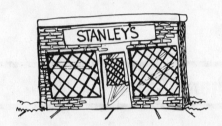

5. A. Tell me about Stanley's Restaurant.

_____ _____ expensive?

B. No, _____. _____.

6. A. Tell me about your neighbors.

_____ _____ noisy?

B. No, _____. _____.

7. A. Tell me about Henry's cat.

_____ _____ pretty?

B. No, _____. _____.

8. A. Tell me about Fred and Sally's dog.

_____ _____ little?

B. No, _____. _____.

9. A. Tell me about the questions in your English book.

_____ _____ difficult?

B. No, _____. _____.

10. A. Tell me about Santa Claus.

_____ _____ thin?

B. No, _____. _____.

The Weather

  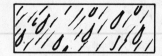 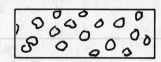

It's sunny.　　It's cloudy.　　It's raining.　　It's snowing.

It's hot.　　It's warm.　　It's cool.　　It's cold.

How's the weather today in YOUR city?

ON YOUR OWN: A Long Distance Telephone Call

A. Hi, Jack. This is Jim. I'm calling from Miami.

B. From Miami? What are you doing in Miami?

A. I'm on vacation.

B. How's the weather in Miami? Is it sunny?

A. No, it isn't. It's raining.

B. Is it hot?

A. No, it isn't. It's cold.

B. Are you having a good time?

A. No, I'm not. I'm having a TERRIBLE time. The weather is TERRIBLE here.

B. I'm sorry to hear that.

A. Hi, _____. This is _____. I'm calling from _____.

B. From _____? What are you doing in _____?

A. I'm on vacation.

B. How's the weather in _____? Is it _____?

A. No, it isn't. It's _____.

B. Is it _____?

A. No, it isn't. It's _____.

B. Are you having a good time?

A. No, I'm not. I'm having a TERRIBLE time. The weather is TERRIBLE here.

B. I'm sorry to hear that.

1. *Switzerland*
cool?
snowing?

2. *Honolulu*
hot?
sunny?

You're on vacation and the weather is terrible. Call a student in your class. Use the conversation above as a guide.

29

CLASSROOM DRAMA: You're A Genius!

	I	am.
Yes,	he / she / it	is.
	we / you / they	are.

	I'm not.	
No,	he / she / it	isn't.
	we / you / they	aren't.

Act this out in class.

To Be: Review
Present Continuous Tense:
 Review
Prepositions of Location

My Favorite Photographs

A. Who is he?

B. He's my father.

A. What's his name?

B. His name is Paul.

A. Where is he?

B. He's in Paris.

A. What's he doing?

B. He's standing in front of the Eiffel Tower.

Using these questions, talk about the following photographs.

> Who is he/she? (Who are they?)
>
> What _____ name (names)?
>
> Where _____?
>
> What _____ doing?

1. *my wife*
in New York
standing in front of the
Statue of Liberty

2. *my son*
in the park
playing soccer

3. *my daughter*
in her bedroom
sleeping

4. *my husband*
at the beach
swimming

5. *my sister and brother*
at our house
standing in front of the fireplace

6. *my mother*
in our living room
sitting on the sofa and
watching TV

7. *my aunt and uncle*
in their dining room
having dinner

8. *my cousin*
in front of his apartment building
washing his car

9. *my grandmother and grandfather*
at my wedding
crying

10. *my cousin*
in the park
sitting on a bench and
feeding the birds

11. *my friend*
sitting on his bed
playing the guitar

12. *my wife's brother**
in Washington
standing in front of the
Washington Monument

13. *my brother's wife†*
in their apartment
painting their living room

14. *my friends*
at my birthday party
singing and dancing

*wife's brother = brother-in-law
†brother's wife = sister-in-law

ON YOUR OWN: Your Favorite Photographs

This is a picture of my brother and me. My brother's name is Carlos. We're sitting in the living room of our apartment. Carlos is playing the piano and I'm playing the guitar.

Bring in your favorite photographs to class. Talk about them with other students. Ask the other students about *their* **favorite photographs.**

Prepositions
There Is/There Are
Singular/Plural:
Introduction

Where's the Restaurant?

A. Where's the restaurant?
B. It's **next to** the bank.

A. Where's the school?
B. It's **between** the library and the park.

A. Where's the supermarket?
B. It's **across from** the movie theater.

A. Where's the post office?
B. It's **around the corner from** the hospital.

1. Where's the park?

2. Where's the bank?

3. Where's the church?

4. Where's the movie theater?

5. Where's the restaurant?

6. Where's the police station?

7. Where's the fire station?

8. Where's the post office?

Is There a Laundromat in This Neighborhood?

A. Excuse me. Is there a laundromat in this neighborhood?*

B. Yes. There's a laundromat on Main Street, next to the supermarket.

*Or: Is there a laundromat nearby?

1. *post office?*

2. *bank?*

3. *movie theater?*

4. *gas station?*

5. *bus station?*

6. *cafeteria?*

7. *drug store?*

8. *library?*

ON YOUR OWN: What's in Your Neighborhood?

Is there . . . ?   Yes, there is.
No, there isn't.

Draw a simple map of your neighborhood. With another student, ask and answer questions about your neighborhoods. Here are some places you can include in your questions:

bakery	church	gas station	police station
bank	clinic	hospital	post office
barber shop	department store	laundromat	restaurant
beauty parlor	doctor's office	library	school
bus station	drug store	movie theater	supermarket
cafeteria	fire station	park	train station

Is There a Stove in the Kitchen?

A. Is there a stove in the kitchen?

B. Yes, there is. There's a very nice stove in the kitchen.

A. Oh, good.

A. Is there a refrigerator in the kitchen?

B. No, there isn't.

A. Oh, I see.

1. *a closet in the bedroom?*
Yes, . . .

2. *an elevator in the building?*
No, . . .

3. *a window in the kitchen?*
Yes, . . .

4. *a fire escape?*
No, . . .

5. *a superintendent in the building?*
No, . . .

6. *a jacuzzi in the bathroom?*
Yes, . . .

How Many Bedrooms Are There in the Apartment?

> How many windows **are there** in the bedroom?
>
> **There's** one window in the bedroom.
> **There are** two windows in the bedroom.

A. Tell me, how many bedrooms are there in the apartment?

B. There are two bedrooms in the apartment.

A. Two bedrooms?

B. Yes. That's right.

1. *windows*
   living room

2. *floors*
   building

3. *closets*
   apartment

4. *apartments*
   building

5. *bathrooms*
   apartment

6. *washing machines*
   basement

ON YOUR OWN: Looking for an Apartment

| a student
a room
an exercise | Yes, there is.
No, there isn't. | students
rooms
exercises | Yes, there are.
No, there aren't. |

You're looking for a new apartment. Another student in your class is the landlord. Ask the landlord about the apartment on page 55.

1. Is there a stove in the kitchen?
2. Is there a refrigerator in the kitchen?
3. Is there a superintendent in the building?
4. Is there an elevator in the building?
5. Is there a fire escape?
6. Is there a TV antenna on the roof?
7. Is there a radiator in every room?
8. Is there a mailbox near the building?
9. Is there a bus stop near the building?
10 Are there any pets in the building?

11. Are there any children in the building?
12. How many rooms are there in the apartment?
13. How many floors are there in the building?
14. How many closets are there in the bedroom?
15. How many windows are there in the living room?

Ask the landlord some other questions.

_____

_____

_____

Are there any problems in the apartment on page 55? Don't ask the landlord! Another student in your class is a tenant in the building. Ask that student.

16. Are there any mice in the basement?
17. Are there any cockroaches in the apartment?

18. Are there any broken windows?
19. Are there any holes in the walls?

Ask the tenant some other questions.

_____

_____

Singular/Plural
Adjectives
This/That/These/Those

Clothing

Practice saying these words and then write them in the chart on the next page.

- hat
- shirt
- tie
- jacket
- watch
- belt
- pants
- sock
- shoe

- earring
- necklace
- blouse
- bracelet
- skirt
- stocking

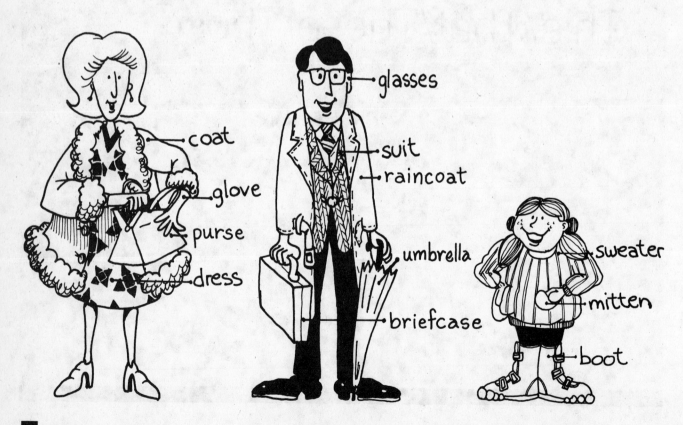

- coat
- glove
- purse
- dress
- glasses
- suit
- raincoat
- umbrella
- briefcase
- sweater
- mitten
- boot

[s]	[z]	[ɪz]
a book – books	a car – cars	a class – classes
a shop – shops	a school – schools	a church – churches
a student – students	a window – windows	a garage – garages
a bank – banks	a store – stores	an exercise – exercises
an airport – airports	an island – islands	an office – offices

a hat—hats

*Some words have irregular plurals:
a man – men
a woman – women
a child – children
a person – people
a tooth – teeth
a mouse – mice

I'm Looking for a Jacket

COLORS

red   orange   yellow   green   blue   purple   black   brown

pink   gray   white   gold   silver

A. May I help you?

B. Yes, please. I'm looking for a jacket.

A. Here's a nice jacket.

B. But this is a PURPLE jacket!

A. That's okay. Purple jackets are very POPULAR this year.

A. May I help you?

B. Yes, please. I'm looking for a _____.

A. Here's a nice _____.

B. But this is a _____ _____!

A. That's okay. _____ _____s are very POPULAR this year.

---

1. *green*

2. *orange*

3. *red*

4. *yellow*

5. *purple*

6. *pink and green*

7. *polka dot*

8. *striped*

46

I'm Looking for a Pair of Gloves

pair of shoes/socks. . . .

A. Can I help you?

B. Yes, please. I'm looking for a pair of gloves.

A. Here's a nice pair of gloves.

B. But these are GREEN gloves!

A. That's okay. Green gloves are very POPULAR this year.

A. Can I help you?

B. Yes, please. I'm looking for a pair of _____.

A. Here's a nice pair of _____.

B. But these are _____ _____s!

A. That's okay. _____ _____s are very POPULAR this year.

1. *pink*

2. *black*

3. *red*

4. *striped*

5. *green and yellow*

6. *purple and brown*

7. *polka dot*

8. *red, white, and blue*

How about YOU?

What are you wearing today?
What are the students in your class wearing today?
What's your favorite color?

47

Excuse Me. I Think That's My Jacket.

This/That is – These/Those are

1. *pen*
2. *pencils*
3. *book*
4. *mittens*
5. *raincoat*
6. *earrings*
7. *sweater*
8.

Lost and Found

A. Is this your umbrella?

B. No, it isn't.

A. Are you sure?

B. Yes. THAT umbrella is brown, and MY umbrella is black.

A. Are these your boots?

B. No, they aren't.

A. Are you sure?

B. Yes. THOSE boots are dirty, and MY boots are clean.

Make up conversations, using colors and other adjectives you know.

1. *watch*

2. *glasses*

3. *purse*

4. *gloves*

5. *little boy*

6. _____

Simple Present Tense

Interviews Around the World

$$\left.\begin{array}{l} \text{I} \\ \text{We} \\ \text{You} \\ \text{They} \end{array}\right\} \text{live.}$$

$$\text{Where do} \left\{\begin{array}{l} \text{I} \\ \text{we} \\ \text{you} \\ \text{they} \end{array}\right\} \text{live?}$$

$$\text{What do} \left\{\begin{array}{l} \text{I} \\ \text{we} \\ \text{you} \\ \text{they} \end{array}\right\} \text{do?}$$

A. What's your name?

B. My name is Antonio.

A. Where do you live?

B. I live in Rome.

A. What language do you speak?

B. I speak Italian.

A. Tell me, what do you do every day?

B. I eat Italian food,
I drink Italian wine,*
and I sing Italian songs!

*Or: coffee, tea, beer, etc.

Interview these people.

What's your name?
Where do you live?
What language do you speak?
What do you do every day?

1. Marie — French — PARIS

2. Carlos — Spanish — MADRID

3. Frieda — German — BERLIN

4. Toshi — Japanese — TOKYO

5. Sara and Mark — English — LONDON

6. Boris and Natasha — Russian — MOSCOW

People Around the World

He / She / It lives.	Where does he / she / it live?	What does he / she / it do?

A. What's his name?

B. His name is Miguel.

A. Where does he live?

B. He lives in Mexico City.

A. What language does he speak?

B. He speaks Spanish.

A. What does he do every day?

B. He eats Mexican food,
he reads Mexican newspapers,
and he listens to Mexican music.

Ask and answer questions about these people.

What's his/her name?
Where does he/she live?
What language does he/she speak?
What does he/she do every day?

1.
   ATHENS — Greek — Anna

2.
   HONG KONG — Chinese — Ming

3.
   SAN JUAN — Spanish — Puerto Rican — Margarita

4.
   TORONTO — English — Canadian — David

5.
   ROME — Italian — Mario

6.
   STOCKHOLM — Swedish — Inga

ON YOUR OWN: A Famous Person

I We You They	live.
He She It	lives.

Where	do	I we you they	live?
	does	he she it	

What	do	I we you they	do?
	does	he she it	

Interview a famous person.

A. What's your name?

B. _____.

A. _____ live?

B. _____.

A. _____ speak?

B. _____.

A. _____ every day?

B. _____.

Now tell the class about this person.

His/Her name is . . .

Simple Present Tense:
Yes/No Questions
Negatives
Short Answers

Stanley's International Restaurant

| He cooks.
He doesn't cook.
(does not) | Does he cook?
Yes, he does.
No, he doesn't. | When }
What kind of food } does he cook? |

Stanley's International Restaurant is a very special place. Every day Stanley cooks a different kind of food. On Monday he cooks Italian food. On Tuesday he cooks Greek food. On Wednesday he cooks Chinese food. On Thursday he cooks Puerto Rican food. On Friday he cooks Japanese food. On Saturday he cooks Mexican food. And on Sunday he cooks American food.

Ask and answer six questions based on this model.

A. What kind of food does Stanley cook **on Monday**?

B. **On Monday** he cooks **Italian** food.

A. Does Stanley cook **Greek** food on **Tuesday**?

B. Yes, he does.

A. Does Stanley cook **Japanese** food on **Sunday**?

B. No, he doesn't.

A. When does he cook **Japanese** food?

B. He cooks **Japanese** food on **Friday**.

You go.
You don't go.
(do not)

Do you go?
Yes, I do.
No, I don't.

When do you go?

A. Do you go to Stanley's Restaurant on **Wednesday**?
B. Yes, I do.
A. Why?
B. Because I like **Chinese** food.

A. Do you go to Stanley's Restaurant on **Sunday**?
B. No, I don't.
A. Why not?
B. Because I don't like **American** food.

A. What kind of food do you like?
B. I like **Russian** food.
A. When do you go to Stanley's Restaurant?
B. I don't go there.
A. Why not?
B. Because Stanley doesn't cook **Russian** food.

Ask these people.

 1. *Friday?*

 2. *Saturday?*

 3. *Monday?*

 4. *Thursday?*

Ask these people.

 5. *Monday?*

 6. *Tuesday?*

 7. *Wednesday?*

 8. *Saturday?*

Ask these people.

 9. *Vietnamese*

 10. *Ethiopian*

 11. *Thai*

 12. *Hungarian*

57

A. What do people do at Stanley's International Restaurant?

B. On Monday they speak Italian, eat Italian food, drink Italian wine, and listen to Italian music.

1. Henry likes Greek food.

When does he go to Stanley's Restaurant?
What does he do there?

2. Alice likes Mexican food.

When does she go to Stanley's Restaurant?
What does she do there?

3. Mr. and Mrs. Wilson go to Stanley's Restaurant on Wednesday.

What kind of food do they like?
What do they do there?

4. What kind of food do YOU like?
When do you go to Stanley's Restaurant?
What do you do there?

ON YOUR OWN: Who Is Your Favorite . . . ?

Answer these questions and then ask other students in your class.

1. a. What kind of movies do you like?
        (Do you like comedies? dramas?
        westerns? adventure movies?
        science fiction movies? cartoons?)

    b. Who is your favorite actor?
        actress?

2. a. What kind of books do you like?
        (Do you like novels? poetry? short
        stories?)

    b. Who is your favorite author?

3. a. What kind of TV programs do you
        like?
        (Do you like comedies? dramas?
        cartoons? game shows? news
        programs?)

    b. Who is your favorite TV star?

4.   What's your favorite food?

5. a. What kind of music do you like?
        (Do you like classical music?
        popular music? jazz? rock music?)

    b. Who is your favorite singer?
        (What kind of songs does he/she
        sing?)

6. a. Which sports do you like?
        (Do you like football? baseball?
        soccer? golf? hockey? tennis?)

    b. Who is your favorite athlete?

CLASSROOM DRAMA: You Speak English Very Well

Yes, { I / we / you / they } do.

{ he / she / it } does.

No, { I / we / you / they } don't.

{ he / she / it } doesn't.

Act this out in class.

Object Pronouns
Simple Present Tense:
  s vs. non-s Endings
Have/Has
Adverbs of Frequency

How Often?

I	me
he	him
she	her
it	it
we	us
you	you
they	them

A. How often does your boyfriend call you?

B. He calls me every night.

1. How often do you speak to your daughter?

every day

2. How often do you write to your son at college?

every week

3. How often do you paint your house?

every year

4. How often do you clean your windows?

every month

5. How often do your grandchildren visit you?

every Sunday

6. How often do you wash your car?

every weekend

7. How often does your boss say "hello" to you?

every day

8. How often do you think about me?

all the time

She Usually Studies in the Library

[s]		[z]		[ɪz]			
eat	eats	read	reads	wash	washes	always	100%
write	writes	bring	brings	watch	watches	usually	90%
bark	barks	call	calls	dance	dances	sometimes	50%
speak	speaks	clean	cleans	fix	fixes	rarely	10%
						never	0%

A. Does Carmen usually study in her room?

B. No. She rarely studies in her room. She usually studies in the library.

1. Does Sally usually eat lunch in the cafeteria?

rarely

outside

2. Does Andrew always watch the news after dinner?

never

game shows

3. Does Irene always read *The National Inquirer?*

never

Time magazine

4. Does Henry usually wash his car on Saturday?

rarely

on Sunday

5. Does your boyfriend sometimes bring you flowers?

never

candy

6. Does your neighbor's dog always bark at night?

never

during the day

We Have Noisy Neighbors

$$\left.\begin{array}{l} \text{I} \\ \text{We} \\ \text{You} \\ \text{They} \end{array}\right\} \text{have}$$

brown eyes.

$$\left.\begin{array}{l} \text{He} \\ \text{She} \\ \text{It} \end{array}\right\} \text{has}$$

A. Do you have quiet neighbors?

B. No. We have noisy neighbors.

1. Do you have a cat?
   a dog

2. Do Mr. and Mrs. Hill have a new car?
   an old car

3. Does this store have an elevator?
   an escalator

4. Do you have a brother?
   a sister

5. Does your daughter have straight hair?
   curly hair

6. Does your baby boy have blue eyes?
   brown eyes

ON YOUR OWN: Very Different

My brother and I look very different. I have brown eyes and he has blue eyes. We both have brown hair, but I have short, curly hair and he has long, straight hair. I'm tall and thin. He's short and heavy.

As you can see, I don't look like my brother. We look very different.

Who in your family do you look like? Who DON'T you look like? Explain.

My sister and I are very different. I'm a teacher. She's a journalist. I live in Chicago. She lives in Paris. I have a small house in the suburbs. She has a large apartment in the city.

I'm married. She's single. I play golf. She plays tennis. I play the piano. She doesn't play a musical instrument. On the weekend I usually watch TV and rarely go out. She never watches TV and always goes to parties.

As you can see, we're very different. But we're sisters . . . and we're friends.

Compare yourself with a member of your family, another student in your class, or a famous person. Explain how you and this person are different.

Contrast:
Simple Present and Present Continuous Tenses
Tenses
Adjectives

I Always Cry When I'm Sad

Why are you crying?

I'm crying because I'm sad.
I ALWAYS cry when I'm sad.

1. Why are you smiling?

_____ happy.

I ALWAYS _____.

2. Why is he shouting?

_____ angry.

He ALWAYS _____.

3. Why is she biting her nails?

_____ nervous.

She ALWAYS _____.

4. Why is the bird drinking?

_____ thirsty.

It ALWAYS _____.

5. Why are they going to
Stanley's Restaurant?

_____ hungry.

They ALWAYS _____.

6. Why is he going to the
doctor?

_____ sick.

He ALWAYS _____.

7. Why are they shivering?

_____ cold.

They ALWAYS _____.

8. Why are you perspiring?

_____ hot.

I ALWAYS _____.

9. Why is she yawning?

_____ tired.

She ALWAYS _____.

10. Why is he blushing?

_____ embarrassed.

He ALWAYS _____.

ON YOUR OWN: What Do You Do When You're Nervous?

What do you do when you're nervous?

Do you perspire?

Do you bite your nails?

Do you walk back and forth?

Answer these questions and then ask another student in your class.

What do you do when you're . . .

1. nervous?

   When I'm nervous I bite my nails.
   _____

2. sad?

   _____

3. happy?

   _____

4. tired?

   _____

5. sick?

   _____

6. cold?

   _____

7. hot?

   _____

8. hungry?

   _____

9. thirsty?

   _____

10. angry?

    _____

11. embarrassed?

    _____

I'm Washing the Dishes in the Bathtub

A. What are you doing?!

B. I'm washing the dishes in the bathtub.

A. That's strange! Do you USUALLY wash the dishes in the bathtub?

B. No. I NEVER wash the dishes in the bathtub, but I'm washing the dishes in the bathtub TODAY.

A. Why are you doing THAT?!

B. Because my sink is broken.

A. I'm sorry to hear that.

A. What are you doing?!

B. I'm _____.

A. That's strange! Do you USUALLY _____?

B. No. I NEVER _____, but I'm _____ TODAY.

A. Why are you doing THAT?!

B. Because my _____ is broken.

A. I'm sorry to hear that.

1. sleep
   sleeping } on the floor
   bed

2. cook
   cooking } on the radiator
   stove

3. study
   studying } English by candlelight
   lamp

4. shout
   shouting } to my neighbor across
   the street

   telephone

5. hitchhike
   hitchhiking } to work
   car

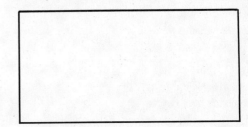

6.

Can
Have to

Can You?

I He She It We You They	} can/can't sing. (cannot)

Can you sing?
Yes, I can.
No, I can't.

 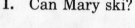 

1. Can Mary ski?

2. Can Sam cook Chinese food?

3. Can they play the violin?

4. Can you sing?

5. Can Jeff play chess?

6. Can William play the piano?

7. Can Sally play football?

8. Can they skate?

9. Ask another student in your class: Can you _____?

Of Course They Can

A. Can Jack fix cars?

B. Of course he can.
He fixes cars every day. He's a mechanic.

1. Can Arthur play the violin?
violinist

2. Can Anita sing?
singer

3. Can Fred and Ginger dance?
dancer

4. Can Stanley cook?
chef

5. Can Lois bake apple pies?
baker

6. Can Richard act?
actor

7. Can Elizabeth and Katherine act?
actress

8. Can Eleanor teach?
teacher

9. Can Shirley drive a truck?
truck driver

They Can't Go to Herbert's Party

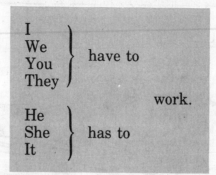

I		
We	have to	
You		work.
They		
He		
She	has to	
It		

Herbert is depressed. He's having a party today, but his friends can't go to his party. They're all busy.

A. Can Michael go to Herbert's party?

B. No, he can't. He has to go to the doctor.

1. *Peggy?*
fix her car

2. *George and Martha?*
go to the supermarket

3. *Nancy?*
go to the dentist

4. *Henry?*
clean his apartment

5. *Carl and Tim?*
do their homework

6. *Linda?*
wash her clothes

7. *Ted?*
go to the bank

8. Can YOU go to Herbert's party?
No, _____.

Make up conversations with other students in your class.

Include some of these words in your questions.

go to a movie
go to a baseball game
have lunch
have dinner
go swimming
go dancing
go skating
go skiing
go shopping
go bowling
go sailing
go jogging

Include some of these words and others in your answers.

go to the doctor
go to the bank
do my homework
visit a friend in the hospital
work

_____
_____
_____
_____
_____
_____
_____

Future: Going to
Time Expressions
Want to

What Are They Going to Do Tomorrow?

(I am)	I'm	
(He is)	He's	
(She is)	She's	
(It is)	It's	going to read.
(We are)	We're	
(You are)	You're	
(They are)	They're	

	am	I	
	is	he / she / it	
What			going to do?
	are	we / you / they	

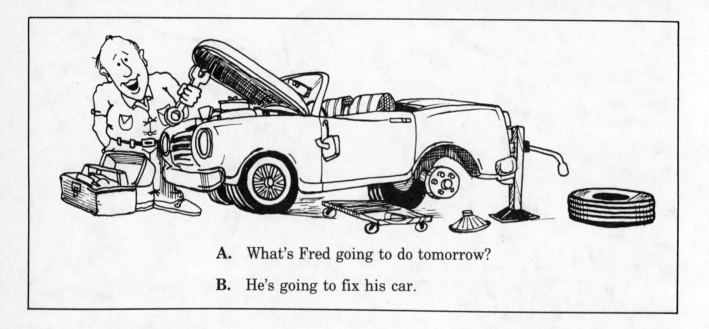

A. What's Fred going to do tomorrow?

B. He's going to fix his car.

1. *Mary*

2. *Carol and Dan*

3. *you*

4. *Tom*

5. *you*

6. *Henry*

They're Going to the Beach

They're going to go to the beach tomorrow. = They're going to the beach tomorrow.

	today	*tomorrow*
	this morning	tomorrow morning
	this afternoon	tomorrow afternoon
	this evening	tomorrow evening
	tonight	tomorrow night

A. What are Mr. and Mrs. Brown going to do tomorrow?

B. They're going (to go) to the beach.

1. What's Jane going to do tomorrow evening?

2. What are Ken and Barbara going to do tonight?

3. What are you going to do this afternoon?

4. What are you and your sister going to do tomorrow morning?

5. What's Ahmed going to do today?

6. What are you going to do tomorrow?

When Are You Going to . . . ?

*Other phrases you can use are:

this/next week, month, year
this/next Sunday, Monday, Tuesday, Wednesday, Thursday, Friday, Saturday
this/next January, February, March, April, May, June, July, August,
            September, October, November, December
this/next spring, summer, fall (autumn), winter

†Or: I'm going to call him right away/immediately/at once.

1. When are you going to wash your car?

2. When are you going to call your grandmother?

3. When are you going to visit us?

4. When are you going to cut your hair?

5. When are you going to plant flowers this year?

6. When are you going to fix your car?

7. When are you going to write to your Uncle John?

8. Mr. Smith! When are you going to iron those pants?

9. Ask another student: When are you going to _____?

What's the Forecast?

A. What are you going to do tomorrow?

B. I don't know. I want to **go swimming,** but I think the weather is going to be bad.

A. Really? What's the forecast?

B. The radio says it's going to **rain.**

A. That's strange! According to the newspaper, it's going to **be sunny.**

B. I hope you're right. I REALLY want to **go swimming.**

1. *have a picnic*
rain
be nice

2. *go skiing*
be warm
snow

3. *go to the beach*
be cloudy
be sunny

4. *plant flowers in my garden*
be very hot
be cool

5. *go sailing*
be foggy
be clear

6. *go to the zoo with my children*
be cold
be warm

Discuss in class.

What's the weather today?
What's the weather forecast for tomorrow?

What Time Is It?

It's 11:00.   It's eleven o'clock.

It's 11:15.   It's eleven fifteen.*

It's 11:30.   It's eleven thirty.*

It's 11:45.   It's eleven forty-five.*

It's 12:00.   It's twelve o'clock.

It's noon.   It's midnight.

*You can also say:

     11:15 – a quarter after eleven
     11:30 – half past eleven
     11:45 – a quarter to twelve

A. What time does the movie begin?

B. It begins at 8:00.

A. At 8:00?! Oh no! We're going to be late!

B. Why? What time is it?

A. It's 7:30! We have to leave RIGHT NOW!

B. I can't leave now. I'm SHAVING!

A. Please try to hurry! I don't want to be late for the movie.

A. What time does _____?

B. It _____ at _____.

A. At _____?! Oh no! We're going to be late!

B. Why? What time is it?

A. It's _____! We have to leave RIGHT NOW!

B. I can't leave now. I'm _____!

A. Please try to hurry! I don't want to be late for the _____.

1. What time does the football game begin?
2:00/1:30
taking a bath

2. What time does the plane leave?
4:15/3:45
putting on my clothes

3. What time does English class begin?
9:00/8:45
getting up

4. What time does the bus leave?
7:00/6:30
packing my suitcase

5. What time does the train leave?
5:15/4:30
taking a shower

6. What time does the play begin?
8:30/8:00
looking for my pants

7. _____

Past Tense:
Regular Verbs
Introduction to
Irregular Verbs

How Do You Feel Today?

I feel great!

I feel fine.

I feel okay.

I'm glad to hear that.

So-so.

Not so good.

I feel terrible.

I'm sorry to hear that.

A. What's the matter?

B. I have a headache.

1. *stomachache*

2. *toothache*

3. *backache*

4. *earache*

5. *sore throat*

6. *cold*

Ask another student in your class.

A. How do you feel today?

B. _____.

A. I'm glad to hear that.

A. How do you feel today?

B. _____.

A. What's the matter?

B. I have _____.

A. I'm sorry to hear that.

What Did You Do Yesterday?

I work every day.

I play the piano every day.

I rest every day.

I work**ed** yesterday.

I play**ed** the piano yesterday.

I rest**ed** yesterday.

work	–	work**ed**	[t]
play	–	play**ed**	[d]
rest	–	rest**ed**	[ɪd]

What did you do yesterday?

[t]

1. *I worked*

2. *cook*

3. *talk on the telephone*

4. *fix*

5. *brush*

6. *dance*

7. *wash*

8. *watch*

[d]

9. *play*

10. *study*

11. *shave*

12. *smile*

13. *clean*

14. *cry*

15. *listen to*

16. *yawn*

[ɪd]

17. *shout*

18. *paint*

19. *wait for*

20. *plant*

What's the Matter?

I
We
You
They } work every day.

He
She
It } works every day.

I
We
You
They
He
She
It } worked yesterday.

A. How does David feel?

B. Not so good.

A. What's the matter?

B. He has a backache.

A. A backache? How did he get it?

B. He played basketball all day.*

*Or: He played basketball all morning/all afternoon/all evening/all night.

1. *Jane*

2. *George*

3. *you*

4. *Mary*

5. *Fred*

6. *you*

7. *Barbara*

8. *Mrs. Smith*

9. *you*

10. *Sally*

11. *Mario*

12. *you*

13. *Helen*

14. *you*

15. *Walter*

ON YOUR OWN: Do You Want to Make an Appointment?

You don't feel very well today. Call your doctor and make an appointment.

A. Hello, Doctor _____? This is
_____.

B. Hello, _____. How are you?

A. I don't feel very well today.

B. I'm sorry to hear that. What seems
to be the problem?

A. I have a TERRIBLE _____.

B. Do you have any idea why?

A. Well, Doctor . . . I _____ all _____
yesterday.

B. I see. Do you want to make an appointment?

A. Yes, please. When can you see me?

B. How about tomorrow at _____ o'clock?

A. That's fine. Thank you very much.

Past Tense:
   Yes/No Questions
   Short Answers
   WH-Questions
   More Irregular Verbs
Time Expressions

I Brushed My Teeth

Today includes:

this morning
this afternoon
this evening
tonight

Yesterday includes:

yesterday morning
yesterday afternoon
yesterday evening
last night

1. Did he study English last night?

2. Did she wash her windows this morning?

3. Did you play the piano yesterday afternoon?

4. Did they call the doctor this afternoon?

5. Did she listen to records yesterday morning?

6. Did he clean his bedroom today?

We Went to the Supermarket

I went.	Did you go?
I didn't go.	Yes, I did.
(did not)	No, I didn't.

Did you go to the bank this afternoon?

No, we didn't. We went to the supermarket.

1. Did you go skating yesterday?
   go – went

2. Did you take the subway this morning?
   take – took

3. Did Steven get up at 10:00 this morning?
   get – got

4. Did he have a stomachache last night?
   have – had

5. Did Mrs. Smith buy bananas yesterday?
   buy – bought

6. Did Tommy write to his grandmother this week?
   write – wrote

7. Did you read a book this afternoon?
   read – read

8. Did they do their homework last night?
   do – did

Mary's Terrible Day

1. Mary went to a party last night.

2. She got up late today.

3. She missed the bus.

4. She had to walk to the office.

5. She arrived late for work.

6. Her boss shouted at her.

7. She had a bad headache all afternoon.

Complete this conversation, using the information above.

A. Hi, Mary! Did you have a good day today?

B. No, I didn't. I had a TERRIBLE day.

A. What happened?

B. I had a bad headache all afternoon.

A. Why did you have a bad headache?

B. Because my boss shouted at me.

A. Why did your boss shout at you?

B. Because I arrived late for work.

A. Why _____ late for work?

B. Because _____ .

A. Why _____ ?

B. Because _____ .

A. Why _____ ?

B. Because _____ .

A. Why _____ ?

B. Because I went to a party last night.

How about YOU?

Did you go to a party last night?
What did you do last night?

Did you get up late today?
What time did you get up?

How did you get to class today?
Did you arrive on time?

Excuses

Are you sometimes late for class?
What do you usually tell your teacher?
Here are some excuses you can use the next time you're late.

I got up late.

I missed the _____. (bus/train/subway)

I had a _____ this morning. (stomachache/headache/...)

I had to go to the _____ before class. (post office/bank/doctor/dentist/...)

I forgot* my _____ and had to go back home and get it. (English book/pencil/...)

I met* _____ on the way to class. (an old friend/my cousin/...)

A thief stole* my _____. (car/bicycle/...)

Add some of your own excuses.

_____

_____

* forget — forgot
  meet — met
  steal — stole

A. I'm sorry I'm late.

B. What happened? Did you get up late?

A. No. I didn't get up late.

B. Did you miss the bus?

A. No. I didn't miss the bus.

B. Well, why are you late?

A. A thief stole my bicycle!

B. Excuses! Excuses!

Now practice this conversation with other students in your class, using your own excuses.

A. I'm sorry I'm late.

B. What happened? Did _____?

A. No. _____.

B. Did _____?

A. No. _____.

B. Well, why are you late?

A. _____.

B. Excuses! Excuses!

To Be: Past Tense

PRESTO Commercials

I He She It	} was	
		happy.
We You They	} were	

Before our family bought PRESTO Vitamins, we were always tired.

I was tired.
My wife was tired.
My children were tired, too.

Now we're energetic, because WE bought PRESTO Vitamins. How about you?

Before our family bought _____, we were always _____.

I was _____.
My wife/husband was _____.
My children were _____, too.

Now we're _____ because WE bought _____. How about you?

Using the above script, prepare commercials for these other fine PRESTO products.

1. sad   happy   2. hungry   full   3. dirty   clean

4. sick   healthy   5. heavy   thin   6. _____ _____

Before I Bought PRESTO Shampoo . . .

Before I bought PRESTO Shampoo, my hair **was** always dirty. Now **it's** clean.

1. Before we bought PRESTO Toothpaste, our teeth _____ yellow. Now _____ white.

2. Before we bought PRESTO Paint, our house _____ ugly. Now _____ beautiful.

3. Before I bought PRESTO Furniture, I _____ uncomfortable. Now _____ very comfortable.

4. Before we bought PRESTO Dog Food, our dog _____ tiny. Now _____ enormous.

5. Before William bought PRESTO Window Cleaner, his windows _____ dirty. Now _____ clean.

6. Before Mr. and Mrs. Brown bought PRESTO Floor Wax, their kitchen floor _____ dull. Now _____ shiny.

7. Before I bought _____,
_____.
Now _____.

Were You at the Ballgame Last Night?

I		
He	}	wasn't
She		(was not)
It		
We		
You	}	weren't
They		(were not)

A. Were you at the ballgame last night?

B. No, I wasn't. I was at the movies.

1. Was it hot yesterday?

2. Were they at home this morning?

3. Was Betty sad yesterday?

4. Was your grandfather a dentist?

5. Were you at home last weekend?

6. Was I a quiet baby?

7. Was Richard on time for his plane?

8. Was Nancy late for the bus?

Did You Sleep Well Last Night?

I He She It We You They } did/didn't	I He She It } was/wasn't We You They } were/weren't

A. Did you sleep well last night?
B. Yes, I did. I was tired.

A. Did Roger sleep well last night?
B. No, he didn't. He wasn't tired.

1. **A.** Did Tom have a big breakfast today?

   B. Yes, _____. _____ hungry.

2. **A.** Did Jane have a big breakfast today?

   B. No, _____. _____ hungry.

3. **A.** Did Mrs. Brown go to the doctor yesterday?

   B. Yes, _____. _____ sick.

4. **A.** Did Mr. Brown go to the doctor yesterday?

   B. No, _____. _____ sick.

5. **A.** Did Timothy finish his milk?

   B. Yes, _____. _____ thirsty.

6. **A.** Did Jennifer finish her milk?

   B. No, _____. _____ thirsty.

7. **A.** Did Susan miss the train?

   B. Yes, _____. _____ late.

8. **A.** Did Sally miss the train?

   B. No, _____. _____ late.

Yes,
$\begin{Bmatrix} I \\ he \\ she \\ it \end{Bmatrix}$ was.
$\begin{Bmatrix} we \\ you \\ they \end{Bmatrix}$ were.

No,
$\begin{Bmatrix} I \\ he \\ she \\ it \end{Bmatrix}$ wasn't.
$\begin{Bmatrix} we \\ you \\ they \end{Bmatrix}$ weren't.

Yes,
$\begin{Bmatrix} I \\ he \\ she \\ it \\ we \\ you \\ they \end{Bmatrix}$ did.

No,
$\begin{Bmatrix} I \\ he \\ she \\ it \\ we \\ you \\ they \end{Bmatrix}$ didn't.

Answer these questions and then ask other students in your class.

1. What did you look like?
   Were you tall? thin? pretty? handsome? cute?
   Did you have curly hair? straight hair? long hair?
   Did you have dimples? freckles?

2. Did you have many friends?
   What did you do with your friends?
   What games did you play?

3. Did you like school?
   Who was your favorite teacher? Why?
   What was your favorite subject? Why?

4. What did you do in your spare time?
   Did you have a hobby?
   Did you play sports?

5. Who was your favorite hero?

6. How old were you when you began to talk?
   (I was _____ years old when I began to talk.)
   What were your first words?
   (My first words were _____.)

7. How old were you when you began to walk?

8. How o' ____ you when you started school?

9. H ____ when you went on your first date?

Add three c ____ ____tudents in your class.

_____?

_____?

_____?

Like to
Review of Tenses:
Simple Present
Simple Past
Future: Going to
Time Expressions
Indirect Object Pronouns

Are You Going to Cook Spaghetti This Week?

A. Are you going to cook spaghetti this week?

B. No, I'm not.   I cooked spaghetti LAST week,* and I don't like to cook spaghetti very often.

*You can also say:
yesterday morning, afternoon, evening
last night
last week, weekend, month, year
last Sunday, Monday, . . . Saturday
last spring, summer, fall (autumn), winter
last January, February, . . . December

1. Are you going to study English this weekend?

2. Are you going to watch TV tonight?

3. Are you going to drink coffee this morning?

4. Is Robert going to buy new clothes this year?

5. Are you going to have dessert this evening?

6. Is Tommy going to play baseball this Saturday?

7. Is Mr. Peterson going to plant flowers this spring?

8. Is Mrs. Johnson going to clean her apartment this week?

9. Are you going skiing* this February?

10. Is Linda going to travel to Canada this August?

11. Are Mr. and Mrs. Smith going to London this summer?

12. Are you and your friends going to Miami this winter?

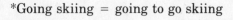

*Going skiing = going to go skiing

What Are You Going to Give Your Wife for Her Birthday?

I'm going to give my wife a present.
I'm going to give   her   a present.

A. What are you going to give your wife for her birthday?

B. I don't know.   I can't give her a necklace.   I gave her a necklace LAST YEAR.

A. How about flowers?

B. No.   I can't give her flowers.   I gave her flowers TWO YEARS AGO.

A. Well, what are you going to give her?

B. I don't know.   I really have to think about it.

A. What are you going to give your _____ for (his/her) birthday?

B. I don't know.   I can't _____.   I _____ LAST YEAR.

A. How about _____?

B. No.   I can't _____.   I _____ TWO YEARS AGO.

A. Well, what are you going to give (him/her)?

B. I don't know.   I really have to think about it.

---

1. *husband*
   a new shirt
   a necktie

2. *girlfriend*
   perfume
   a bracelet

3. *boyfriend*
   a belt
   a sweater

4. *grandmother*
   flowers
   candy

5. *daughter*
   a bicycle
   a doll

6.

Harry!   I'm Really Upset!

> Harry! I'm really upset!
> Do you know what day this was?
> It was my birthday, Harry.   And you forgot again.
> You didn't send me flowers.
> You didn't give me candy.
> You didn't buy me a present.
> And you didn't even wish me "Happy Birthday."

> Happy Birthday, Gladys!

> I love you, Harry!

Why Was She Upset with Harry?

1. He didn't _____ flowers.
2. _____ candy.
3. _____ a present.
4. _____ "Happy Birthday."

ON YOUR OWN: Birthdays

January 23rd = January twenty-third
November 16th = November sixteenth
December 31st = December thirty-first

When is your birthday?
(My birthday is _____.)

Tell about your last birthday:

What did you do?

Did you receive any presents?

What did you get?

Did your family or friends do anything special for you?

What did they do?

Count/Non-Count Nouns

What's in Henry's Kitchen?

Count Nouns	Non-Count Nouns
tomatoes	*cheese*
eggs	*milk*
bananas	*ice cream*
apples	*bread*

Add foods from YOUR kitchen.

Let's Make Sandwiches for Lunch!

Let's make sandwiches for lunch!

Sorry, we can't. There **isn't** any **bread**.

Let's make an apple pie for dessert!

Sorry, we can't. There **aren't** any **apples**.

1. **A.** Let's make a salad for dinner!
   B. Sorry, _____. _____ lettuce.

2. **A.** Let's make an omelette for breakfast!
   B. Sorry, _____. _____ eggs.

3. **A.** Let's make some fresh lemonade!
   B. Sorry, _____. _____ lemons.

4. **A.** Let's bake a cake for dessert!
   B. Sorry, _____. _____ flour.

5. **A.** Let's make pizza for lunch!
   B. Sorry, _____. _____ cheese.

6. **A.** Let's make some fresh orange juice for breakfast!
   B. Sorry, _____. _____ oranges.

7. **A.** Let's make chicken and rice for dinner!
   B. Sorry, _____. _____ chicken.

8. **A.** Let's have french fries with our hamburgers!
   B. Sorry, _____. _____ potatoes.

9. **A.** Let's _____!
   B. Sorry, _____. _____.

How Much Milk Do You Want?

how much?	how many?
too much	too many
a little	a few

A. How much milk do you want?

B. Not too much.   Just a little.

A. Okay.   Here you are.

B. Thanks.

A. How many cookies do you want?

B. Not too many.   Just a few.

A. Okay.   Here you are.

B. Thanks.

1. *coffee*

2. *french fries*

3. *ice cream*

4. *rice*

5. *meatballs*

6.

ON YOUR OWN: Would You Care for Some More?

A. How do you like the _____?

B. I think (it's/they're) delicious.

A. I'm glad you like (it/them). Would you care for some more?

B. Yes, please. But not (too much/too many). Just (a little/a few).
My doctor says that (too much/too many)_____ (is/are) bad for my health.

Practice this conversation with other students in your class, using these foods and others.

1. *potatoes*

2. *chocolate cake*

3. *ice cream*

4. *cookies*

5.

20

Partitives
Count/Non-Count Nouns
Imperatives

Do We Need Anything from the Supermarket?

My Shopping List

a can of beans
a jar of jam
a bottle of soda
a box of cereal
a bag of flour
a loaf of white bread
2 loaves of whole wheat bread
a bunch of bananas
2 bunches of carrots
a head of lettuce

a lb.* of butter
½ lb.* of cheese

a quart of milk
a dozen eggs

*A lb. = a pound; ½ lb. = a half pound, or half a pound.

A. Do we need anything from the supermarket?

B. Yes.   We need a loaf of bread.

A. A loaf of bread?

B. Yes.

A. Anything else?

B. No.   Just a loaf of bread.

1. *cereal*

2. *jam*

3. *soda*

4. *bananas*

5. *vegetable soup*

6. *whole wheat bread*

7. *flour*

8.

 How about YOU?

What did YOU buy the last time you went shopping?

118

How Much Does a Head of Lettuce Cost?

A. How much does **a head of lettuce** cost?

B. **Ninety-five cents** (95¢).*

A. NINETY-FIVE CENTS?!   That's a lot of money!

B. You're right.   **Lettuce** is very expensive this week.

*25¢ = twenty-five cents
 50¢ = fifty cents
       etc.

A. How much does **a pound of apples** cost?

B. **A dollar twenty-five** ($1.25).†

A. A DOLLAR TWENTY-FIVE?!   That's a lot of money!

B. You're right.   **Apples** are very expensive this week.

†$1.00 = a dollar $2.25 = two twenty-five
 $1.50 = a dollar fifty $4.50 = four fifty
                etc.

1. *butter*

2. *carrots*

3. *milk*

4. *onions*

5. *Swiss cheese*

6. *soda*

7. *white bread*

8. *oranges*

9.

What Would You Like?

A. What would you like **for dessert?**

B. I can't decide. What do you recommend?

A. I recommend our **chocolate ice cream.** Everybody says **it's** delicious.*

B. Okay. Please give me **a dish of chocolate ice cream.**

A. What would you like **for breakfast?**

B. I can't decide. What do you recommend?

A. I recommend our **scrambled eggs.** Everybody says **they're** out of this world.*

B. Okay. Please give me **an order of scrambled eggs.**

*You can also say: fantastic, wonderful, magnificent, excellent.

What would you like . . .

1. . . . for dessert?
(a piece of) apple pie

2. . . . for lunch?
(a bowl of) chicken soup

3. . . . to drink?
(a cup of) coffee

4. . . . for breakfast?
(an order of) pancakes

5. . . . to drink?
(a glass of) red wine

6. . . . for dessert?
(a dish of) vanilla ice cream

7. . . . to drink?
(a cup of) hot chocolate

8. . . . for dessert?
(a bowl of) strawberries

9.

Stanley's Favorite Recipes

Are you going to have a party soon?   Do you want to cook something special?   Stanley the chef recommends this recipe for VEGETABLE STEW.   This is Stanley's favorite recipe for vegetable stew, and everybody says it's fantastic!

1. Put **a little butter** into a saucepan.

2. Chop up **a few onions**.

3. Cut up (**a little / a few**) _____.

4. Pour in _____.

5. Slice _____.

6. Add _____.

7. Chop up _____.

8. Slice _____.

9. Add _____.

10. Cook for 3 hours.

When is your English teacher's birthday?   Do you want to bake a special cake?   Stanley the chef recommends this recipe for FRUITCAKE.   This is Stanley's favorite recipe for fruitcake, and everybody says it's out of this world!

1. Put 3 cups of flour into a mixing bowl.

2. Add **a little sugar**.

3. Slice (**a little / a few**) _____.

4. Cut up _____.

5. Pour in _____.

6. Add _____.

7. Chop up _____.

8. Add _____.

9. Mix in _____.

10. Bake for 45 minutes.

How about YOU?

Do you have a favorite recipe?
Share it with other students in your class.

21

Future Tense: Will
Time Expressions
Might

Will the Train Arrive Soon?

(I will) I'll	
(He will) He'll	
(She will) She'll	
(It will) It'll } work.	
(We will) We'll	
(You will) You'll	
(They will) They'll	

Will he work?
Yes, he will.

A. Will the train arrive soon?

B. Yes, it will. It'll arrive in five minutes.

1. Will the soup be ready soon?
Yes, _____. _____ in a few minutes.

2. Will Miss Blake return soon?
Yes, _____. _____ in an hour.

3. Will Dr. Smith be here soon?
Yes, _____. _____ in half an hour.

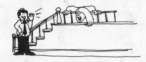

4. Will you be ready soon?
Yes, _____. _____ in a few seconds.

5. Will the tomatoes be ripe soon?
Yes, _____. _____ in a few weeks.

6. Will the concert begin soon?
Yes, _____. _____ at seven o'clock.

7. Will Mrs. Green be home soon?
Yes, _____. _____ in a little while.

8. Will you be back soon?
Yes, _____. _____ in a week.

9. Will Betty get out of the hospital soon?
Yes, _____. _____ in a few days.

10. Will Frank get out of jail soon?
Yes, _____. _____ in a few months.

What Do You Think?

I		
He		
She		
It	will	work.
We		
You		
They		

I		
He		
She		
It	won't	work.
We	(will not)	
You		
They		

Do you think it'll rain tomorrow?

Maybe it will, and maybe it won't. We'll just have to wait and see.

1. Do you think Cynthia will marry Norman?

2. Do you think it'll be very cold this winter?

3. Do you think you'll be happy in your new neighborhood?

4. Do you think Mary's husband will find a new job?

5. Do you think I'll be famous some day?

6. Do you think they'll have a baby soon?

7. Do you think there will be many people at the beach tomorrow?

8. Do you think we'll have to fight in a war some day?

9. Do you think _____?

They Really Can't Decide

A. When are you going to clean your apartment?

B. I don't know.   I might clean it today, or I might clean it next Saturday.   I really can't decide.

A. Where are you going to go for your vacation?

B. We don't know.   We might go to Mexico, or we might go to Japan.   We really can't decide.

1. What is he going to cook tonight?

2. What color is she going to paint her kitchen?

3. What are they going to name their new daughter?

4. When are you two going to get married?

5. What are you going to buy your brother for his birthday?

6. What are they going to do tonight?

7. How are you going to come to class tomorrow?

8. What's he going to name his new puppy?

9. What are you going to be when you grow up?

Careful!

A. Careful! Put on your helmet!

B. I'm sorry. What did you say?

A. Put on your helmet! You might hurt your head.

B. Oh. Thanks for the warning.

1. The floor is wet!
fall

2. Don't stand there!
get hit

3. Don't smoke in here!
start a fire

4. Put on your safety glasses!
hurt your eyes

5. Don't touch the machine!
get hurt

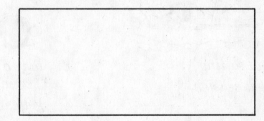

6.

I'm Afraid I Might Drown

A. Would you like to go swimming with me?*

B. No, I don't think so.

A. Why not?

B. I'm afraid I might drown.

A. Don't worry!   You won't drown.

B. Are you sure?

A. I'm positive!

B. Okay.   I'll go swimming with you.

*Or: Do you want to go swimming with me?

1. *go skiing*
    break my leg

2. *go to a fancy restaurant*
    get sick

3. *go to the beach*
    get a sunburn

4. *go dancing*
    step on your feet

5. *take a walk in the park*
    catch a cold

6. *go to Jack's party*
    have a terrible time

7. *go sailing*
    get seasick

8. *take a ride in the*
    country
    get carsick

9. *go to the movies*
    fall asleep

10. _____

22

Comparatives
Should
Possessive Pronouns

My New Apartment Is Larger

cold – colder short – shorter	large – larger safe – safer	big – bigger hot – hotter	easy – easier busy – busier

A. I think you'll like my new apartment.

B. But I liked your OLD apartment. It was **large**.

A. That's right. But my new apartment is **larger**.

1. *bicycle*
   fast

2. *refrigerator*
   big

3. *dog*
   friendly

4. *neighborhood*
   safe

5. *living room rug*
   soft

6. *sports car*
   fancy

7. *tennis racket*
   light

8. *recipe for vegetable stew*
   easy

9. *wig*
   pretty

My New Rocking Chair Is More Comfortable

A. I think you'll like my new rocking chair.

B. But I liked your OLD rocking chair.   It was **comfortable**.

A. That's right.   But my new rocking chair is **more comfortable**.

1. *girlfriend*
   intelligent

2. *boyfriend*
   handsome

3. *house*
   beautiful

4. *kitchen sink*
   large

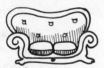

5. *sofa*
   attractive

6. *English teacher*
   smart

7. *roommate*
   interesting

8. *boss*
   nice

9. *computer*
   powerful

10. *air conditioner*
    quiet

11. *recipe for fruitcake*
    delicious

12.

Bicycles Are Safer Than Motorcycles

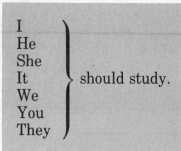

I
He
She
It
We
You
They
} should study.

Should I study?

A. Should I buy a bicycle or a motorcycle?

B. I think you should buy a bicycle.

A. Why?*

B. Bicycles are **safer than** motorcycles.

A. Should he study English or Latin?

B. I think he should study English.

A. Why?*

B. English is **more useful than** Latin.

---

*Or: Why do you say that? What makes you say that? How come?

1. Should I buy a dog or a cat?

2. Should he buy a used car or a new car?

3. Should I vote for John Black or Peter Smith?

4. Should he go out on a date with Doris or Jane?

5. Should she go out on a date with Roger or Bill?

6. Should they buy a black-and-white TV or a color TV?

7. Should we buy this fan or that fan?

8. Should she buy these earrings or those earrings?

9. Should I plant flowers or vegetables this spring?

10. Should he study the piano with Mrs. Wong or Miss Schultz?

11. Should I buy the hat in my left hand or the hat in my right hand?

12. Should they go to the cafeteria up the street or the cafeteria down the street?

13. Should she buy fur gloves or leather gloves?

14. Should I go to the laundromat across the street or the laundromat around the corner?

15. Should I hire Miss Jones or Miss Wilson?

16. Should I fire Mr. Jackson or Mr. Brown?

17.

Don't Be Ridiculous!

my – mine	our – ours
his – his	your – yours
her – hers	their – theirs

A. You know, my dog isn't as friendly as your dog.

B. Don't be ridiculous!   Yours is MUCH friendlier than **mine**.

A. You know, my novels aren't as interesting as Ernest Hemingway's novels.

B. Don't be ridiculous!   Yours are MUCH more interesting than **his**.

fast

1. *my car*
    your car

comfortable

2. *my furniture*
    your furniture

nice

3. *my boss*
    your boss

intelligent

4. *my children*
    your children

big

5. *my house*
    the Jones's house

clean

6. *my apartment*
    your apartment

good-better

7. *my pronunciation*
    Maria's pronunciation

important

8. *my job*
    the President's job

9.

In my opinion, New York is more interesting than San Francisco.

I disagree. I think San Francisco is MUCH more interesting than New York.

Do you think the weather in Miami is better than the weather in Honolulu?

No, I don't think so. I think the weather in Honolulu is MUCH better than the weather in Miami.

Are the people in Centerville as friendly as the people in Greenville?

No, but they're more interesting. Don't you agree?

Yes, I agree.

| _____er than |
| more _____ than |

as _____ as
not as _____ as

Talk with other students about two cities: your home town and the city you live in now, or any two cities you know. Talk about . . .

the streets: quiet, safe, clean, wide, busy . . . ?
the buildings: high, modern, pretty . . . ?
the weather: cold, warm, rainy, snowy . . . ?
the people: friendly, nice, polite, honest, busy, happy, hospitable,
        talkative, healthy, wealthy, poor . . . ?
the city in general: large, interesting, lively, exciting, expensive . . . ?

In your conversation you might want to use some of these expressions:

Do you think . . . ?
Don't you agree?

I agree.
I disagree.
I agree/disagree with (you, him, her, John . . .).

I think so.
I don't think so.
In my opinion, . . .

Superlatives

The Smartest Person I Know

kind – the kindest cold – the coldest	nice – the nicest safe – the safest
busy – the busiest happy – the happiest	big – the biggest hot – the hottest

A. I think your friend Margaret is very **smart**.

B. She certainly is.   She's **the smartest** person I know.

1. *your cousin*
friendly

2. *your Uncle George*
funny

3. *your parents*
kind

4. *your older brother*
shy

5. *your cousin Nancy*
pretty

6. *Larry*
lazy

7. *the students in our class*
nice

8. *your Aunt Gertrude*
cold

9. *your younger brother*
sloppy

The Most Energetic Person I Know

A. I think your grandmother is very **energetic.**

B. She certainly is.   She's **the most energetic** person I know.

1. *your son*
   polite

2. *John*
   stubborn

3. *our English teacher*
   patient

4. *your older sister*
   bright

5. *your younger sister*
   talented

6. *your upstairs neighbor*
   noisy

7. *your downstairs neighbor*
   boring

8. *your twin brothers*
   nice

9. *your grandfather*
   generous

10. *Walter*
    stingy

11. *your girlfriend*
    honest

12.

139

I Want to Buy a Small Radio

a small radio
a smaller radio
the smallest radio

a comfortable chair
a more comfortable chair
the most comfortable chair

a good car
a better car
the best car

A. May I help you?

B. Yes, please. I want to buy a **small** radio.

A. I think you'll like this one. It's VERY **small.**

B. Don't you have a **smaller** one?

A. No, I'm afraid not. This is **the smallest** one we have.

B. Thank you anyway.

A. Sorry we can't help you. Please come again.

A. May I help you?

B. Yes, please. I want to buy a/an _____ _____.

A. I think you'll like this one. It's VERY _____.

B. Don't you have a/an { _____er | more _____ } one?

A. No, I'm afraid not. This is the { _____est | most _____ } one we have.

B. Thank you anyway.

A. Sorry we can't help you. Please come again.

1. *large refrigerator*

2. *comfortable rocking chair*

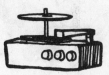

3. *good record player*

4. *fancy necktie*

5. *cheap watch*

6. *small kitchen table*

7. *good tape recorder*

8. *light tennis racket*

9. *elegant evening gown*

10. *modern sofa*

11. *short novel*

12.

good	bad
better	worse
best	worst

Ask and answer these questions with another student in your class. Give reasons for your opinions.

In your opinion . . .

1. Who is the most popular actor/actress in your country?

2. Who is the most popular TV star?

3. Who is the best singer? (What kind of songs does he/she sing?)

4. Who is the most important person in your country now? (What does he/she do?)

5. Who is the most important person in the history of your country? (What did he/she do?)

In your opinion . . .

6. What is the best city in your country? Why?

7. What is the worst city in your country? Why?

8. What are the most interesting tourist sights for visitors to your country? (museums, monuments, churches . . .)

9. What are the most popular vacation places for people in your country? Why?

In your opinion . . .

10. What is the most popular car in your country?

11. What is the most popular sport?

12. What is the funniest TV program?

13. What is the best newspaper?

14. What is the most popular magazine?

15. What is the most popular food?

Directions

Can You Tell Me How to Get to the Laundromat from Here?

walk up
walk down
walk along

on the right
on the left

next to
across from
between

laundromat?

A. Excuse me. Can you tell me how to get to the laundromat from here?

B. Sure. **Walk up** Main Street and you'll see the laundromat **on the right, across from** the drug store.

A. Thank you.

post office?

A. Excuse me. Can you tell me how to get to the post office from here?

B. Sure. **Walk down** Main Street and you'll see the post office **on the left, next to** the high school.

A. Thank you.

1. *shoe store?*

2. *police station?*

3. *high school?*

4. *barber shop?*

5. *butcher shop?*

6. *bank?*

Could You Please Tell Me How to Get to the Hospital from Here?

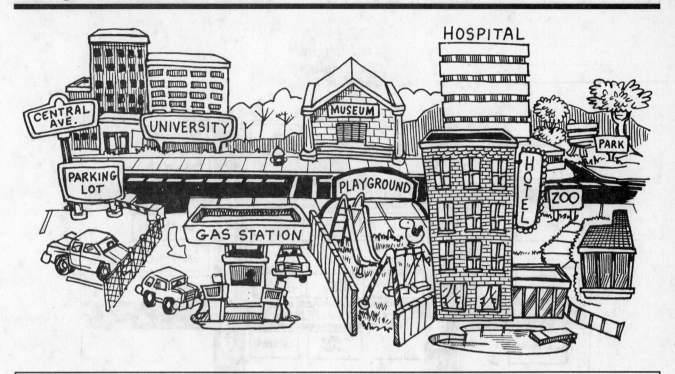

hospital?

A. Excuse me.   Could you please tell me how to get to the hospital from here?

B. Sure.   **Walk along** Central Avenue and you'll see the hospital **on the left, between** the museum and the park.

A. Thanks.

1. *parking lot?*

2. *university?*

3. *park?*

4. *museum?*

5. *playground?*

6. *zoo?*

Would You Please Tell Me How to Get to the Bus Station from Here?

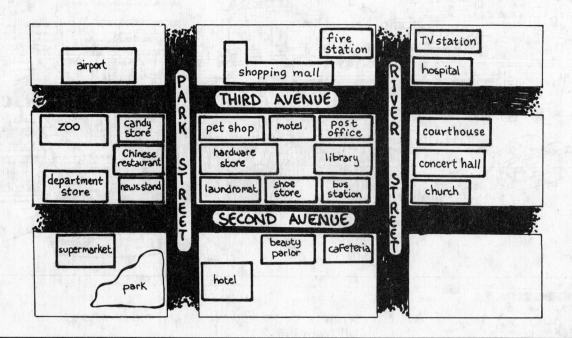

turn right
turn left

bus station?

A. Excuse me. Would you please tell me how to get to the bus station from here?

B. Certainly. **Walk up** Park Street to Second Avenue and **turn right.** **Walk along** Second Avenue and you'll see the bus station **on the left, across from** the cafeteria.

A. Thanks very much.

concert hall?

A. Excuse me. Would you please tell me how to get to the concert hall from here?

B. Certainly. **Drive along** Second Avenue to River Street and **turn left.** **Drive up** River Street and you'll see the concert hall **on the right, between** the courthouse and the church.

A. Thanks very much.

1. *shopping mall?*

2. *hardware store?*

3. *library?*

4. *zoo?*

5. *department store?*

6. TV *station?*

7. *hospital?*

8.

Take the Main Street Bus and Get Off at First Avenue

A. Excuse me.   What's the quickest way to get to Peter's Pet Shop?

B. **Take** the Main Street bus and **get off** at First Avenue.
Walk up First Avenue and you'll see Peter's Pet Shop **on the right**.

A. Thank you very much.

B. You're welcome.

A. Excuse me.   What's the easiest way to get to Harry's Barber Shop?

B. **Take** the subway and **get off** at Fourth Avenue.
Walk down Fourth Avenue and you'll see Harry's Barber Shop
on the left.

A. Thank you very much.

B. You're welcome.

1. What's the fastest way to get to the baseball stadium?

2. What's the best way to get to St. Andrew's Church?

3. What's the most direct way to get to the zoo?

4. I'm in a hurry!   What's the shortest way to get to the train station?

ON YOUR OWN: Can You Tell Me How to Get There?

A. Can you recommend **a good hotel**?

B. Yes.   The Bellview is **a good hotel.**   I think it's **one of the best hotels** in town.

A. Can you tell me how to get there?

B. Sure.   Take the subway and get off at Brighton Boulevard.   You'll see the Bellview at the corner of Brighton Boulevard and Twelfth Street.

A. Thank you very much.

B. You're welcome.

These people are visiting your city.   Using the conversation as a guide, recommend real places you know and like, and give directions.

1.   Can you recommend a good restaurant?

2.   Can you recommend a cheap department store?

3.   Can you recommend a quiet, romantic café?

4.   Can you recommend _____?

Adverbs
Comparative of Adverbs
Agent Nouns
If-Clauses

He Drives Very Carelessly

slow – slowly bad – badly beautiful – beautifully	terrible – terribly miserable – miserably simple – simply	sloppy – sloppily busy – busily lazy – lazily	fast – fast hard – hard
			good – well

work – a worker
play – a player
drive – a driver

A. I think he's **a careless driver.**

B. I agree.   He **drives VERY carelessly.**

1. *a careless skier*

2. *a slow chess player*

3. *a beautiful singer*

4. *sloppy painters*

5. *an accurate translator*

6. *a good teacher*

7. *careful workers*

8. *a graceful dancer*

9. *good tennis players*

10. *dishonest card players*

11. *a fast driver*

12. *a hard worker*

He Should Try to Speak More Slowly

softly – { more softly / softer }	carefully – more carefully
loud(ly) – { more loudly / louder }	politely – more politely
slowly – { more slowly / slower }	hard – harder
neatly – { more neatly / neater }	fast – faster
	early – earlier
	late – later

A. Bob speaks VERY **quickly.**

B. You're right.   He should try to speak { **more slowly** / **slower** }.

1. Linda speaks very softly.

2. Ronald goes to bed very late.

3. Janet skates very carelessly.

4. Your friends come to class very early.

5. David types very slowly.

6. They dress very sloppily.

7. Peter speaks to his parents very impolitely.

8. Karen plays her record player very loud.

9. They work very slowly.

If _____ will _____

A. What are they going to name their new baby?

B. If they have a boy, they'll name him John.
If they have a girl, they'll name her Jane.

1. A. How are you going to get to school tomorrow?

B. If it rains, I'll _____.
If it's sunny, I'll _____.

2. A. What's Bob going to do this Saturday afternoon?

B. If the weather is good, he'll _____.
If the weather is bad, he'll _____.

3. A. What's Carmen going to have for dinner tonight?

B. If she's very hungry, _____.
If she isn't very hungry, _____.

4. A. What's Fred going to do tomorrow?

B. If he feels better, _____.
If he doesn't feel better, _____.

5. A. When are you going to go to sleep tonight?

B. If I'm tired, _____.
If I'm not tired, _____.

6. A. What are they going to wear tomorrow?

B. If it's hot, _____.
If it's cool, _____.

How about YOU?

What are you going to do tonight if you have a lot of homework?
What are you going to do tonight if you DON'T have a lot of homework?

What are you going to have for breakfast tomorrow if you're very hungry?
What are you going to have for breakfast tomorrow if you AREN'T very hungry?

What are you going to do this weekend if the weather is nice?
What are you going to do this weekend if the weather is bad?

If You Drive Too Fast, You Might Have an Accident

If _____ might _____

A. You know . . . you shouldn't drive so fast.

B. Oh?

A. Yes.   If you drive too fast, you might have an accident.

B. Hmm.   You're probably right.

1. *work so slowly*
lose your job

2. *sing so loud*
get a sore throat

3. *worry so much*
get an ulcer

4. *eat so much candy*
get a toothache

5. *do your homework so*
carelessly
make too many mistakes

6. *go to bed so late*
be tired in the
morning

7. *use those headphones*
so often
hurt your ears

8. *watch so many scary*
TV *programs*
have nightmares

9.

Many people believe that you'll have GOOD luck

> if you find a four-leaf clover.
> if you find a horseshoe.
> if you give a new pair of shoes to a poor person.

You'll have BAD luck

> if a black cat walks in front of you.
> if you walk under a ladder.
> if you open an umbrella in your house.
> if you put your shoes on a table.

Here are some other superstitions.

> If your right eye itches, you'll laugh soon.
> If your left eye itches, you'll cry soon.
>
> If your right ear itches, somebody is saying good things about you.
> If your left ear itches, somebody is saying bad things about you.
>
> If a knife falls, a man will visit soon.
> If a fork falls, a woman will visit soon.
> If a spoon falls, a baby will visit soon.
>
> If you break a mirror, you'll have bad luck for seven years.
>
> If you spill salt, you should throw a little salt over your left shoulder.
> If you don't, you'll have bad luck.

Do you know any superstitions? Share them with other students in your class.

Past Continuous Tense
Reflexive Pronouns
While-Clauses

The Blackout

I
He
She
It } was

We
You
They } were

working.

Last night at 8:00 there was a blackout in Centerville.   The lights went out all over town.

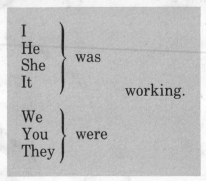

A. What was Doris doing last night when the lights went out?

B. She was taking a bath.

A. What were Mr. and Mrs. Green doing last night when the lights went out?

B. They were riding in an elevator.

Ask about these people.

1. *Ted*

2. *Irene*

3. *Bob and Judy*

4. *you*

5. *Joe*

6. *your parents*

7. *your younger sister*

8. *your father*

9. *Mr. and Mrs. Jones*

What were YOU doing last night at 8:00?

I Saw You Yesterday, but You Didn't See Me

A. I saw you yesterday, but you didn't see me.

B. Really?   When?

A. At about 2:30.   You were **getting out of a taxi on Main Street.**

B. That wasn't me.   Yesterday at 2:30 I was **cooking dinner.**

A. Hmm.   I guess I made a mistake.

1. *walking into the post office*
   fixing my car

2. *walking out of the laundromat*
   cleaning my apartment

3. *getting on a bus*
   watching TV

4. *getting off a merry-go-round*
   playing baseball

5. *jogging through the park*
   playing tennis

6. *riding your bicycle along Main Street*
   cooking

7. *getting out of a police car*
   sleeping

8.

159

He Went to the Movies by Himself

I	myself
you	yourself
he	himself
she	herself
it	itself
we	ourselves
you	yourselves
they	themselves

A. What did **John** do yesterday?

B. He went to the movies.

A. Oh. Who did he go to the movies with?

B. Nobody. He went to the movies **by himself.**

1. *Patty*
   go to the beach

2. *Peter*
   go to the ballgame

3. *you*
   go bowling

4. *you and your wife*
   play cards

5. *Susan and Robert*
   have a picnic

6. *you*
   go to Bob's party

7. *Mrs. Wilson*
   drive to New York

8. *Mr. Wilson*
   take a walk in the park.

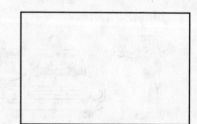

9.

I Had a Bad Day Today

while

A. You look upset.

B. I had a bad day today.

A. Why?   What happened?

B. I **lost my wallet** while I was **jogging through the park.**

A. I'm sorry to hear that.*

A. Harry looks upset.

B. He had a bad day today.

A. Why?   What happened?

B. He **cut himself** while he was **shaving.**

A. That's too bad.*

*Or: How awful!   That's terrible!   What a shame!   What a pity!

1. *you*

   burned myself
   cooking dinner

2. *Sheila*

   dropped her packages
   walking out of the
   supermarket

3. *Tom*

   hurt himself
   playing basketball

4. *your parents*
got a flat tire
driving over a bridge

5. *you*
fainted
waiting for the bus

6. *Nelson*
saw a few gray hairs
looking at himself in
the mirror

7. *you and your wife*
had an accident
driving home

8. *Linda*
cut herself
slicing a tomato

9. *you*
a dog bit me
standing on the corner

10. *Marvin*
tripped and fell
walking to work

11. *your aunt and uncle*
somebody stole their car
shopping

12. *you*
a can of paint fell on me
walking under a ladder

How about YOU?

Everybody has a bad day once in a while.   Try
to remember a few days when something bad
happened to you.   What happened, and what were
you doing when it happened?

27

Could
Be Able to
Have Got to
Too + Adjective

They Couldn't

I	
He	
She	
It	could/couldn't study.
We	
You	
They	

Could he study?
Yes, he could.
No, he couldn't.

A. Could Peter play on the basketball team when he was a little boy?

B. No, he couldn't. He was too **short**.

1. Could Henry go to work yesterday?
sick

2. Could Rita go out with her boyfriend last weekend?
busy

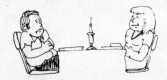

3. Could Mr. and Mrs. Jones finish their dinner?
full

4. Could Billy get into the movie last Saturday night?
young

5. Could you finish your homework last night?
tired

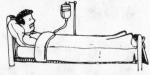

6. Could Frank get out of bed the day after his operation?
weak

7. Could Betty tell the policeman about her accident?
upset

8. Could Stuart eat at his wedding?
nervous

They Weren't Able to

$$\text{could} = \left\{ \begin{array}{l} \text{was} \\ \text{were} \end{array} \right\} \text{able to}$$

$$\text{couldn't} = \left\{ \begin{array}{l} \text{wasn't} \\ \text{weren't} \end{array} \right\} \text{able to}$$

A. Was Jimmy able to lift his grandmother's suitcase?

B. No, he wasn't able to. It was too **heavy.**

1. Was Louise able to paint her house yesterday afternoon?

windy

2. Was Carl able to sit down on the bus this morning?

crowded

3. Were Mr. and Mrs. Johnson able to go swimming in the ocean during their vacation?

cold

4. Was Shirley able to finish her order of spaghetti and meatballs?

spicy

5. Was Tom able to find his wallet last night?

dark

6. Were you able to do the grammar exercises last night?

difficult

7. Were Jeff and Gloria able to see the full moon last night?

cloudy

8. Was Willy able to wear his brother's suit to the dance last Saturday night?

small

She Had to Study for an Examination

A. Did Barbara enjoy herself at the concert last night?

B. Unfortunately, she $\left\{ \begin{array}{c} \text{wasn't able to} \\ \text{couldn't} \end{array} \right\}$ go to the concert last night.   She had to **study for an examination.**

1. Did Ronald enjoy himself at the baseball game yesterday?

go to the dentist

2. Did you enjoy yourself at the tennis match last week?

visit my boss in the hospital

3. Did Mr. and Mrs. Wilson enjoy themselves at the symphony yesterday evening?

wait for the plumber

4. Did Sally enjoy herself at the theater last Saturday night?

take care of her little brother

5. Did Fred enjoy himself at Mary's party last Friday evening?

work late at the office

6. Did you and your classmates enjoy yourselves at the movies last night?

study English

7. Did Marion enjoy herself at the picnic last Sunday?

take care of her neighbor's dog

8. Did you enjoy yourself at the football game yesterday?

fix a flat tire

9. _____

I'm Afraid I Won't Be Able to Help You

will/won't be able to

I've We've You've They've }	got to	=	I We You They }	have to
He's She's It's }	got to	=	He She It }	has to work.

A. I'm afraid I won't be able to help you **move to your new apartment** tomorrow.

B. You won't?   Why not?

A. I've got to **take my son to the doctor.**

B. Don't worry about it!   I'm sure I'll be able to **move to my new apartment** by myself.

1. *clean your garage*
   go to the office

2. *paint your living room*
   fly to Chicago

3. *fix your car*
   drive my husband to the clinic

4. *do your homework*
   practice the piano

5. *repair your kitchen window*
   take care of my neighbor's baby

6. *cook Christmas dinner*
   buy presents for my children

7. *study for the examination*
   take my sister to her ballet lesson

8. *take Jennifer to the dentist*
   work overtime at the factory

9. *take Rover to the vet*
   visit my mother in the hospital

10.

1. George is upset.   He got a flat tire, and he won't be able to get to the airport on time.

2. Rita is frustrated.   She lost her key, and she can't get into her apartment.

3. Mrs. Brown's English class is really upset.   Mrs. Brown is sick, and she won't be able to teach them English this week.

4. Sidney is disappointed.   He wasn't able to find a job in New York City, and he had to move home with his mother and father.

5. Ted was really disappointed last year.   He couldn't dance in the school play.   His teacher said he was too clumsy.

Are you frustrated, disappointed, or upset about something?   Tell the class about your problem.   If you don't have a problem now, tell the class about the LAST time you were frustrated, disappointed, or upset.

28

Must
Must vs. Should
Count/Non-Count Nouns
Past Tense Review

Diets

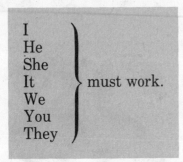

more/less	more/fewer
bread	cookies
fish	potatoes
fruit	eggs

Henry's Diet ⊖	⊕
bread	fish
cookies	vegetables
candy	fruit
potato chips	
other snack foods	

1. Henry had his yearly checkup today.   The doctor told him he's a little too heavy and put him on this diet:

    He must eat **less** bread, **fewer** cookies, **less** candy, and **fewer** potato chips and other snack foods.

    Also, he must eat **more** fish, **more** vegetables, and **more** fruit.

Shirley's Diet ⊖	⊕
fatty meat	lean meat
potatoes	grapefruit
rice	green vegetables
rich desserts	

2. Shirley also had her annual checkup today.   Her doctor put her on this diet:

    She must eat _____

    _____

    _____

Arthur's Diet	
⊖	⊕
butter	margarine
eggs	skim milk
cheese	yogurt
ice cream	

3. Arthur was worried about his heart. He went to his doctor for an examination, and the doctor told him to eat fewer fatty foods.

He must eat/drink_____

_____

_____

Rover's Diet	
⊖	⊕
fatty meat	lean meat
dog biscuits	water

4. Rover went to the vet yesterday for his yearly checkup. The vet told him he's a little too heavy and put him on this diet:

He must eat/drink_____

_____

_____

⊖ MY DIET ⊕	

5. You went to the doctor today for your annual physical examination. The doctor told you you're a little overweight and said you must go on a diet.

I must eat/drink_____

_____

_____

I Must Lose Some Weight

must/mustn't (must not)

A. I had my yearly checkup today.

B. What did the doctor say?

A. He/She told me I'm a little too heavy and I must lose some weight.

B. Do you have to stop eating _____?

A. No, but I mustn't eat as (much/many)_____ as I did before.

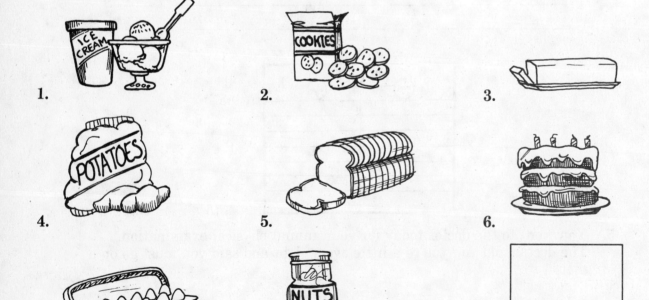

1.

2.

3.

4.

5.

6.

7.

8.

9.

The Checkup

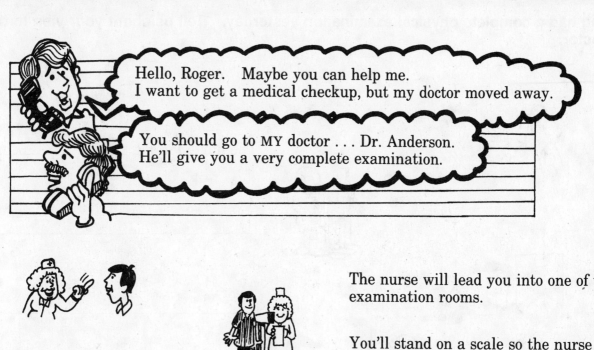

1.  The nurse will lead you into one of the examination rooms.

2. 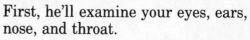 You'll stand on a scale so the nurse can measure your height and your weight.

3. The nurse will leave, and you'll take off your clothes and put on a hospital gown.

4.  Dr. Anderson will come in, shake your hand, and say "hello."

5. First, he'll examine your eyes, ears, nose, and throat.

6. Then, he'll listen to your heart with a stethoscope.

7.  Next, he'll take your pulse.

8.  Then, he'll take your blood pressure.

9.  After that, he'll draw some blood for a blood test.

10.  Finally, he'll take a chest X-ray and do a cardiogram.

Your Checkup

You had a complete physical examination yesterday.　Tell us about your visit to the doctor.

1.

        The nurse **led** me _____.

2.

        _____.

3.

        _____.

4.

        _____.

5.

        _____.

6.

        _____.

7.

        _____.

8.

        _____.

9.

        _____.

10.

        _____.

Really, Doctor?

A. I'm really worried about your heart.

B. Really, Doctor?   Should I stop eating rich desserts?

A. Mr. Jones!   You MUST stop eating rich desserts!   If you don't, you're going to have serious problems with your heart some day.

A. I'm really worried about your _____.

B. Really, Doctor?   Should I _____?

A. (Mr./Miss/Mrs./Ms.) _____!   You MUST _____!
If you don't, you're going to have serious problems with
your _____ some day.

1. *lungs*
stop smoking

2. *back*
start doing exercises

3. *feet*
stop jogging

4. *blood pressure*
take life a little easier

5. *hearing*
*stop listening to loud
rock music*

6.

What do YOU do when you burn your finger?

Some people rub butter on their finger.

Other people put a piece of ice on their finger.

Other people put their finger under cold water.

Different people have different remedies for medical problems that aren't very serious. The following people need your advice. Help them with their medical problems and share your "home remedies" with the other students in your class.

1. I have a cold. What should I do?

2. I have a toothache. What should I do?

3. I have a stomachache. What should I do?

4. I have a bloody nose. What should I do?

5. I have the hiccups. What should I do?

Future Continuous Tense
Time Expressions

Will They Be Home This Evening?

(I will)	I'll
(He will)	He'll
(She will)	She'll
(It will)	It'll
(We will)	We'll
(You will)	You'll
(They will)	They'll

} be working.

A. Will you be home this evening?

B. Yes, I will.   I'll be reading.

1. *Sharon*

2. *Steven*

3. *Mr. and Mrs. Williams*

4. *Bob*

5. *you*

6. *Kathy*

7. *Jack*

8. *you*

9. *Mrs. McDonald*

10. *you and your brother*

11. *Dave*

12. *you*

Hi, Gloria. This Is Arthur.

A. Hi, Gloria. This is Arthur.
Can I come over and visit this evening?

B. No, Arthur. I'm afraid I won't be home this evening. I'll be shopping at the supermarket.

A. Oh. Can I come over and visit TOMORROW evening?

B. No, Arthur. I'm afraid I won't be home tomorrow evening. I'll be working late at the office.

A. I see. Can I come over and visit this WEEKEND?

B. No, Arthur. I'll be visiting my sister in New York.

A. Oh. Well, can I come over and visit next Wednesday?

B. No, Arthur. I'll be visiting my uncle in the hospital.

A. How about sometime next SPRING?

B. No, Arthur. I'll be getting married next spring.

A. Oh!!

B. Good-bye.

When Can You Come Over?

Complete this conversation and practice with another student.

I'm having some problems with the homework for tomorrow.

I'll be glad to help.
When can you come over?

I can come over at _____ o'clock.
Is that okay?

I'm afraid I won't be home at _____ o'clock.
I'll be _____ing.   How about _____ o'clock?

No, I won't be able to come over at _____ o'clock.
I'll be _____ing.   How about _____ o'clock?

Fine.   I'll see you then.

How Long Will Your Aunt Gertrude Be Staying with Us?

A. How long will your Aunt Gertrude be staying with us?

B. She'll be staying with us **for a few months.**

1. How long will they be staying in San Francisco?

until Friday

2. How much longer will you be working on my car?

for a few more hours

3. How late will your husband be working tonight?

until 10 o'clock

4. Where will you be getting off?

at the last stop

5. How much longer will you be practicing the piano?

for a few more minutes

6. How late will your daughter be studying this evening?

until 8 o'clock

7. When will we be arriving in London?

at 7 A.M.

8. How much longer will you be reading?

until I finish this chapter

9. How far will we be driving today?

until we reach Detroit

10. How soon will Santa Claus be coming?

in a few days

Will You Be Home Today at About Five O'Clock?

A. Hello, Richard. This is Julie. I want to return the tennis racket I borrowed from you last week. Will you be home today at about five o'clock?

B. Yes, I will. I'll be cooking dinner.

A. Oh. Then I won't come over at five.

B. Why not?

A. I don't want to disturb you. You'll be cooking dinner!

B. Don't worry. You won't disturb me.

A. Okay. See you at five.

A. Hello, _____. This is _____. I want to return the _____ I borrowed from you last week. Will you be home today at about _____ o'clock?

B. Yes, I will. I'll be _____ing.

A. Oh. Then I won't come over at _____.

B. Why not?

A. I don't want to disturb you. You'll be _____ing!

B. Don't worry. You won't disturb me.

A. Okay. See you at _____.

1. *dictionary*
doing the laundry

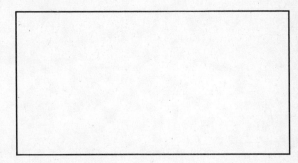

2. *videotape*
watching my favorite TV program

3. *hammer*
helping my son with his homework

4. *coffee pot*
knitting

5. *football*
ironing

6.

30

Some/Any
Pronoun Review
Verb Tense Review

I'll Be Glad to Help

I	me	my	mine	myself
you	you	your	yours	yourself
he	him	his	his	himself
she	her	her	hers	herself
it	it	its	its	itself
we	us	our	ours	ourselves
you	you	your	yours	yourselves
they	them	their	theirs	themselves

A. What's **Johnny** doing?

B. **He's** getting dressed.

A. Does **he** need any help? I'll be glad to help **him**.

B. No, that's okay.   **He** can get dressed by **himself.**

1. *your husband fix the TV*

2. *your daughter feed the canary*

3. *your children cook breakfast*

4. *you and your husband clean the garage*

5. *your sister fix her car*

6. *your son take out the garbage*

7. *Bobby and Billy clean their bedroom*

8. *you do my homework*

9.

I Just Found This Watch

A. I just found this watch.   Is it yours?

B. No, it isn't mine.   But it might be **Fred's.**
He lost **his** a few days ago.

A. Really?   I'll call **him** right away.

B. When you talk to **him,** tell **him** I said "Hello."

1. *umbrella*
   Susan's

2. *briefcase*
   John's

3. *purse*
   Maria's

4. *wallet*
   George's

5. *camera*
   Mr. and Mrs. Green's

6. *notebook*
   Margaret's

7. *ring*
   Albert's

8. *cassette player*
   Bobby and Billy's

9. *address book*
   Edward's

10. *sneakers*
    Helen's

11. *glasses*
    Elizabeth's

12.

I Couldn't Fall Asleep Last Night

A. You look tired today.

B. Yes, I know.   I couldn't fall asleep last night.

A. Why not?

B. My **neighbors** were **arguing**.

A. How late did they **argue**?

B. Believe it or not, they **argued** until 3 A.M.!

A. That's terrible!   Did you call and complain?

B. No, I didn't.   I don't like to complain.

A. Well, I hope you sleep better tonight.

B. I'm sure I will.   My **neighbors** don't **argue** very often.

1. *neighbor's son*
practice the violin

2. *neighbor's dog*
bark

3. *neighbor's daughter
listen to her stereo*

4. *upstairs neighbors
play cards*

5. *downstairs neighbors
dance*

6. *neighbor across the hall
sing*

7. *next door neighbors
clean their apartment*

8. *neighbor's daughter
play the piano*

9. *neighbor's son
lift weights*

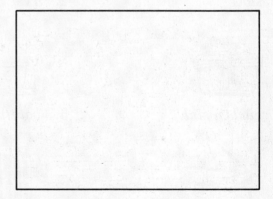

10.

There's Something Wrong with My Washing Machine

something	anything
{ somebody someone }	{ anybody anyone }

A. There's something wrong with my **washing machine**.

B. I'm sorry.   I can't help you.   I don't know ANYTHING about **washing machines**.

A. Do you know anybody who can help me?

B. Not really.   You should look in the phone book.*   I'm sure you'll find somebody who can fix it.

*Or: You should look in the Yellow Pages.

1. *stove*

2. *TV*

3. *refrigerator*

4. *kitchen sink*

5. *bathtub*

6. *dishwasher*

7. *piano*

8. *radiator*

9.

Can You Send a Plumber?

A. Armstrong Plumbing Company.   Can I help you?

B. Yes.   There's something wrong with my kitchen sink.   Can you send a plumber to fix it as soon as possible?

A. Where do you live?

B. 156 Grove Street in Centerville.

A. I can send a plumber tomorrow morning.   Is that okay?

B. Not really.   I'm afraid I won't be home tomorrow morning.   I'll be taking my son to the dentist.

A. How about tomorrow afternoon?

B. Tomorrow afternoon?   What time?

A. Between one and four.

B. That's fine.   Somebody will be here then.

A. What's the name?

B. Helen Bradley.

A. And what's the address again?

B. 156 Grove Street in Centerville.

A. And the phone number?

B. 237–9180.

A. Okay.   We'll have someone there tomorrow afternoon.

B. Thank you.

A. _____. Can I help you?

B. Yes. There's something wrong with my _____. Can you send a _____ to fix it as soon as possible?

A. Where do you live?

B. _____ in _____.

A. I can send a _____ tomorrow morning. Is that okay?

B. Not really. I'm afraid I won't be home tomorrow morning. I'll be _____ing.

A. How about tomorrow afternoon?

B. Tomorrow afternoon? What time?

A. Between _____ and _____.

B. That's fine. Somebody will be here then.

A. What's the name?

B. _____.

A. And what's the address again?

B. _____ in _____.

A. And the phone number?

B. _____.

A. Okay. We'll have someone there tomorrow afternoon.

B. Thank you.

1. *General Radio and TV Service*
repair person

2. *Acme Electrical Repair*
electrician

3. *Patty's Plumbing and Heating*
plumber

ON YOUR OWN: That's What Friends Are For!

    Frank has some very nice friends.   He sees his friends often.
When he needs help, they're always happy to help him.   For example,
last week Frank moved to a new apartment.   He couldn't move
everything by himself, and he didn't really have enough money to hire a
moving company.   His friends came over and helped him move
everything.   He was very grateful.   His friends said, "We're happy to
help you, Frank.   That's what friends are for!"

    Emma has some very special friends.   She sees her friends often.
When she needs help, they're always happy to help her.   For example,
last month the faucet broke in Emma's kitchen and flooded her
apartment.   There was water in every room.   She couldn't fix
everything by herself, and her superintendent didn't help her at all.
Her friends came over and helped her fix the faucet and clean up every
room in the apartment.   She was very grateful.   Her friends said,
"We're happy to help you, Emma.   That's what friends are for!"

**It's nice to have friends you can rely on when you need help.   Tell about a time when
your friends helped you.   Tell about a time when you helped a friend.**

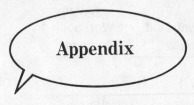

Appendix

Cardinal Numbers

1	one	20	twenty
2	two	21	twenty-one
3	three	22	twenty-two
4	four	.	.
5	five	.	.
6	six	29	twenty-nine
7	seven	30	thirty
8	eight	40	forty
9	nine	50	fifty
10	ten	60	sixty
11	eleven	70	seventy
12	twelve	80	eighty
13	thirteen	90	ninety
14	fourteen		
15	fifteen	100	one hundred
16	sixteen	200	two hundred
17	seventeen	300	three hundred
18	eighteen	.	.
19	nineteen	.	.
		900	nine hundred
		1,000	one thousand
		2,000	two thousand
		3,000	three thousand
		.	.
		.	.
		10,000	ten thousand
		100,000	one hundred thousand
		1,000,000	one million

Ordinal Numbers

1st	first	20th	twentieth
2nd	second	21st	twenty-first
3rd	third	22nd	twenty-second
4th	fourth	.	.
5th	fifth	.	.
6th	sixth	29th	twenty-ninth
7th	seventh	30th	thirtieth
8th	eighth	40th	fortieth
9th	ninth	50th	fiftieth
10th	tenth	60th	sixtieth
11th	eleventh	70th	seventieth
12th	twelfth	80th	eightieth
13th	thirteenth	90th	ninetieth
14th	fourteenth		
15th	fifteenth	100th	one hundredth
16th	sixteenth	1,000th	one thousandth
17th	seventeenth	1,000,000th	one millionth
18th	eighteenth		
19th	nineteenth		

How to read a date:
June 9, 1941 = "June ninth, nineteen forty-one"

Irregular Verbs: Past Tense

be	was	feel	felt	light	lit	sleep	slept
begin	began	fight	fought	lose	lost	speak	spoke
bite	bit	find	found	make	made	stand	stood
break	broke	fly	flew	meet	met	steal	stole
bring	brought	forget	forgot	put	put	sweep	swept
buy	bought	get	got	read	read	swim	swam
catch	caught	give	gave	ride	rode	take	took
come	came	go	went	run	ran	teach	taught
cut	cut	grow	grew	say	said	tell	told
do	did	have	had	see	saw	think	thought
drink	drank	hear	heard	sell	sold	throw	threw
drive	drove	hurt	hurt	send	sent	understand	understood
eat	ate	know	knew	shake	shook	wear	wore
fall	fell	lead	led	sing	sang	write	wrote
feed	fed	leave	left	sit	sat		

Correlation Key to Activity Workbooks

Student Text Pages	Activity Workbook 1 Pages	Student Text Pages	Activity Workbook 1 Pages	Student Text Pages	Activity Workbook 1 Pages
Chapter 1		**Chapter 8**		**Chapter 13**	
2	1-4	44-45	50-52 (A,B,C,D)	74	91-92 (A,B)
Chapter 2		46	52 (E)	75	92-94 (C,D,E,F,G)
6-7	5	47	53	76	95-96
8	6-8	48	54-56	77	97-98
9	9-11	49	57-58	**Chapter 14**	
Chapter 3		**Check-Up Test**	59-60	80	99-100
12-13	12	**Chapter 9**		82-83	101-102 (D,E)
14-15	13-18	52	61-62 (A)	84	102-106 (F,G,H,I,J,K,L)
Check-Up Test	19	53	62-64 (B,C,D)	85-86	107-109
Chapter 4		54	65-67	**Check-Up Test**	110-111
18	20	**Chapter 10**		**Chapter 15**	
19-20	21-24	56	68-69	88	112-113
21	25-26	57	70	89	114-115
Chapter 5		58	71-72	90-91	116-119
24-25	27	59	73	**Chapter 16**	
26-27	28-31	**Check-Up Test**	74	94	120-121
28	32-34	**Chapter 11**		95	122-124 (D,E,F)
Chapter 6		62	75-76 (A)	96	124 (G)
32-34	35-38	63	76-78 (B,C,D,E,F)	97-98	125-126
Check-Up Test	39	64	79	**Chapter 17**	
Chapter 7		65	80-81	100	127
36	40	**Chapter 12**		101	128
37	41	68	82-85	102	129
38	42-44	70-71	86-89	103	130-131
39-40	45	**Check-Up Test**	90	104	132-134
41-42	46-49			**Check-Up Test**	135-136

Student Text Pages	Activity Workbook 2 Pages	Student Text Pages	Activity Workbook 2 Pages	Student Text Pages	Activity Workbook 2 Pages
Chapter 18		**Chapter 23**		**Chapter 27**	
106-107	1-6	138	54	164	93-94
108	7-8	139	55-57	165	95
109	9-10	140-141	58-61	166	96-97 (D,E)
				167-168	97-99 (F,G,H)
Chapter 19		**Check-Up Test** 62-63		169	99-100 (I,J,K)
112	11-12				
113	13-15 (C,D,E)	**Chapter 24**		**Check-Up Test** 101-102	
114	15-17 (F,G)	144	64		
115	18-21	145	65	**Chapter 28**	
		146-147	66-68	172-173	103-105
Chapter 20		148	69-70	174	106-107
118	22-23	149	71	175-176	108
119	23-25 (B,C,D)			177	109-110
120	26-28	**Chapter 25**			
121	29	152	72-74	**Chapter 29**	
		153	75-76	180	111
Check-Up Test 30-31		154	77-79	181-182	112-113
		155	80	183	114-116
Chapter 21		156	81	184-185	117-119
124	32				
125	33-35	**Check-Up Test** 82-83		**Chapter 30**	
126	36			188	120-121 (A)
127	37	**Chapter 26**		189	121-122 (B,C)
128	38-40	158	84-85 (A,B,C)	190-191	122-124 (D)
		159	86-88 (D,E,F)	192	124-126 (E, F)
Chapter 22		160	89 (G)	193-194	126-130 (G,H,I,J,K)
130	41	161-162	89-92 (H,I,J,K)		
131	42			**Check-Up Test** 131-132	
132-133	43-48				
134	49-51				
135	52-53				

Index

A

A/an, 45
A few, 114-115, 121
A little, 114-115, 121
Able to, 165-169
Adjectives, 24-29, 68-69
    comparative of, 130-135, 140-141
    superlative of, 138-142, 148-149
Adverbs, 152-153, 155
    comparative of, 153
    of frequency, 63
Agent nouns, 152
Any, 113, 192-194
As + adjective + as, 134-135

B

Because, 57

C

Can/can't, 74-77
Clothing, 44-49
Colors, 46-49
Comparative:
    of adjectives, 130-135
    of adverbs, 153
Could/couldn't, 164, 166, 169
Count/non-count nouns, 112-115, 121,
    172-174

D

Dates, 109
Days of the week, 56
Did/didn't, 94-98, 103-104
Directions, 144-149
Do/does, 52-60

F

Fewer, 172-173

G

Going to + verb, 80-86, 106-108, 126

H

Had to, 166
Have, 64-65
Have got to, 167-168
Have to, 76-77
How many, 40, 42, 114
How much, 114, 119

I

If, 154-156
Imperatives, 121, 127
Indirect object pronouns, 108-109
Irregular nouns, 45
Irregular verbs, 91, 95, 97, 175-176

L

Less, 172-173
Like, 57-59

Like to, 106-107

M

Many, 40, 42, 114, 174
May I, 46-47
Maybe, 125
Might, 126-128, 155, 189
Months, 82, 106-107
Much, 114-115, 174
Must, 172-174, 177
    must vs. have to, 174
    must vs. should, 177

N

Nationalities, 52-58
Nouns:
    count/non-count, 112-115, 121,
    172-174
    singular/plural, 39-49

O

Object pronouns, 62, 189, 195
Or, 24-25, 132-133

P

Pair of, 47
Partitives, 118-120
Plural, 40, 42, 45-49
Possessive adjectives, 18-21
Possessive nouns, 24-25, 27, 189
Possessive pronouns, 134, 189
Prepositions of location, 32-38, 144-149
Pronouns:
    indirect object, 108-109
    object, 62, 189, 195
    possessive, 134, 189
    reflexive, 160-162, 188, 195
    review of, 188-189, 195
    subject, 7-8
Pronunciation:
    of -ed endings, 89
    of s-endings, 45, 63

Q

Quantity:
    a few, 114-115, 121
    a little, 114-115, 121
    a lot of, 119, 154
    fewer, 172-173
    less, 172-173
    many, 40, 42, 114, 174
    much, 114-115, 174
    some, 118, 192
Questions:
    yes/no questions:
        with simple present tense, 56-57,
        60
        with "to be" present, 19-20, 24-29
    WH-questions:
        with simple present tense, 56-59
        with "to be" present, 7-21, 32-34

R

Reflexive pronouns, 160-162, 188, 195

S

Seasons, 82, 106-107
Should, 132-133, 155, 177-178
Singular/plural, 39-49
Some, 118, 192
Superlatives, 138-142, 148-149

T

Telephone numbers, 2
Tenses:
    future continuous, 180-185
    future: going to, 80-86, 106-108, 126
    future: will, 124-125, 128, 154
    past continuous, 158-159, 161-162,
        190-191
    present continuous, 12-21, 32-34, 68,
        70-71
    review of tenses, 106-107, 175-176,
        190-194
    simple past, 89-104
    simple past vs. past continuous,
        161-162, 190-191
    simple present, 52-60
    simple present vs. present
        continuous, 68, 70-71
There is/there are, 37-42
This/that/these/those, 48-49
Time, 85-86
Time expressions, 80-83, 94-95,
    106-108, 124, 126, 183
To Be:
    past tense, 100-104
    present tense, 7-15
    short answers:
        positive, 19-20, 30
        negative, 26-30
    yes/no questions, 26-29
Too + adjective, 164-165
Too + adverb, 155

U

Until, 183

W

Want to, 84
Weather, 28-29
What, 12
What kind of, 56-59
When, 56-58
Where, 7, 9
While-clauses, 161-162
Who, 32-34
Why, 57
Would you, 115, 120, 128, 146-147